“In this hi[illegible]ppropriately provocative book, Joanie Connell has captured essential tips for today’s youth and for the parents who want them to succeed, along with vivid examples of what does and does not work. I couldn’t put her book down, and will come back to it again and again for clear and well-founded reminders of the fundamentals that I and my kids need to apply to live and work more authentically, productively, and effectively. Flying without a Helicopter is full of straightforward, practical common sense that is seemingly not too common these days.”

—Bernardo M. Ferdman, Ph.D., Distinguished Professor of Organizational Psychology, Alliant International University, and editor of Diversity at Work: The Practice of Inclusion

“This book should be required reading for any parent who wants to ‘help’ their child in the workplace. I will be sending it to the dad who contacted me to set up an interview for his Ivy-league graduate son.”

—Alexandra Watkins, author of Hello My Name Is Awesome: How to Create Brand Names That Stick and Chief Innovation Officer at Eat My Words

Connell shows us how to be good stewards of our most valuable asset: human capital. Flying without a Helicopter deals with the perennial “us versus them” attitude that has always existed among the generations. She tackles the issue candidly and effectively and provides us with shocking insights regarding expectations versus reality. The solutions provided are compelling and vital to our success as a nation if we are to continue to be trusted leaders in a global economy.”

—Christina de Vaca, Director of the Master of Science in Executive Leadership program at the University of San Diego

"Dr. Connell's descriptions and concerns about an entitled, passive generation reflect those of many in the psychotherapy community. In my own practice, I hear from intelligent, well-educated parents with material means and position about how hard it is for them to see their children in discomfort. Can't there be as much learned in failing as in succeeding, in losing as in winning? As more and more professionals become enlightened about the issues that Dr. Connell highlights, we all stand to benefit and to, hopefully, reconsider what 'help' looks like."

—Martha A. Hayes, Licensed Clinical Social Worker (LCSW)

"Assumptions and stereotypes about younger workers abound. They become one more hurdle for younger workers to jump as they strive to succeed at work. Joanie Connell's book—Flying Without a Helicopter—helps parents, educators, and managers cut through the myths and labels young people have today and gives practical tips to help them succeed at work."

—Julie O'Mara, author and consultant
specializing in Diversity and Inclusion

"Joanie Connell's book Flying without a Helicopter: How to Prepare Young People for Work and Life is a much-needed guide for parents, employers, managers, and young people themselves. Connell delivers a highly functional blend of her academic, experiential, and practical knowledge into a compelling book of deep thought, compassionate engagement, and useful exercises. Highly recommended!"

—Flip Brown, author of Balanced Effectiveness at Work: How to
Enjoy the Fruits of Your Labor without Driving Yourself Nuts

Flying without a Helicopter

How to Prepare Young People for Work and Life

Joanie B. Connell, Ph.D.

Tamar & Larry
Have a nice flight!
Joanie

FLYING WITHOUT A HELICOPTER
HOW TO PREPARE YOUNG PEOPLE FOR WORK AND LIFE

iUniverse books may be ordered through booksellers or by contacting:

iUniverse
1663 Liberty Drive
Bloomington, IN 47403
www.iuniverse.com
1-800-Authors (1-800-288-4677)

ISBN: 978-1-4917-5264-7 (sc)
ISBN: 978-1-4917-5263-0 (hc)
ISBN: 978-1-4917-5265-4 (e)

Library of Congress Control Number: 2014919645

Printed in the United States of America.

iUniverse rev. date: 12/11/2014

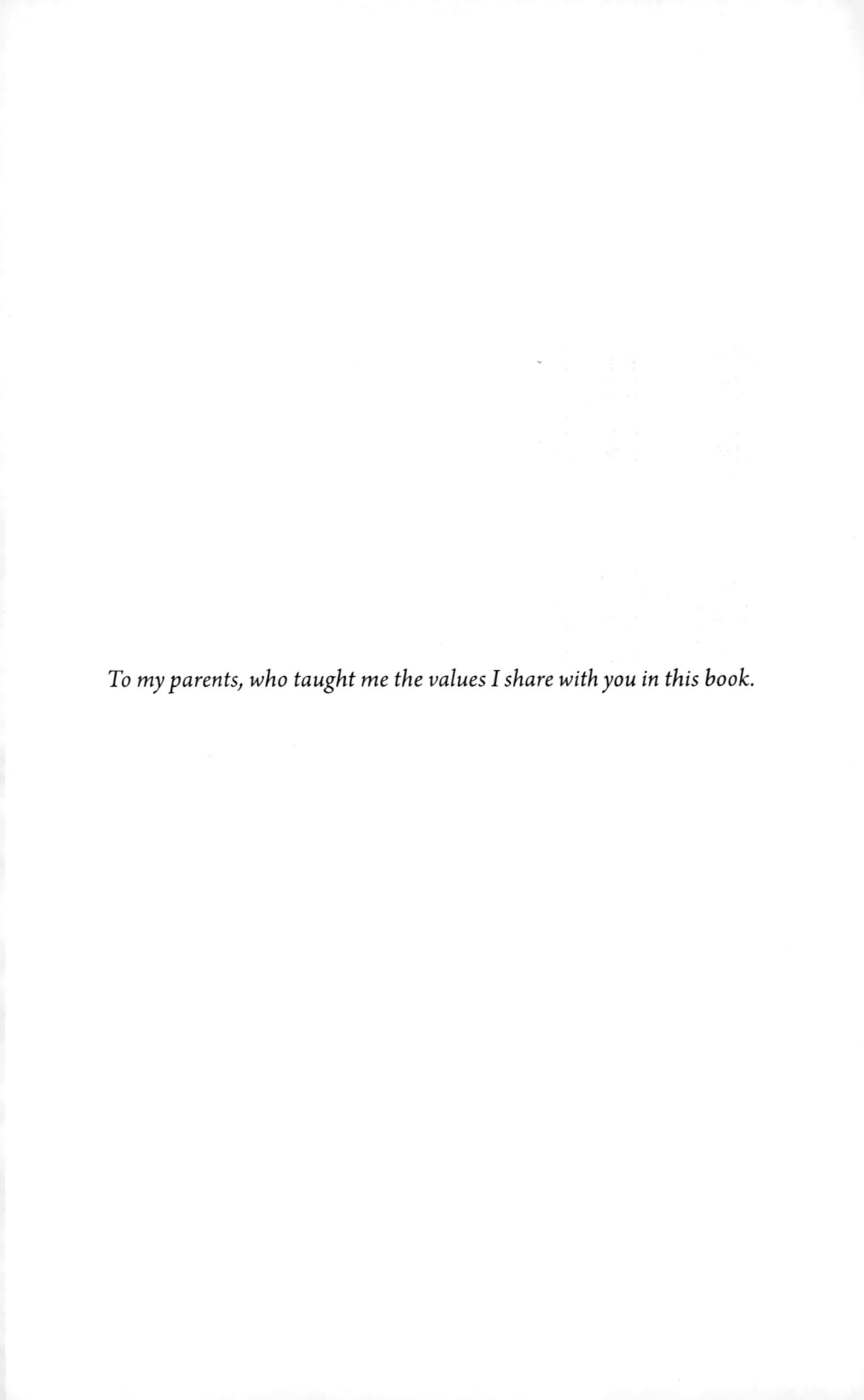

To my parents, who taught me the values I share with you in this book.

CONTENTS

Part 2: Solutions

Part 3: Exercises

FOREWORD

In *Flying without a Helicopter: How to Prepare Young People for Work and Life,* Joanie Connell has provided a convincing analysis and well-reasoned approaches, which address one of education's most challenging problems. With seemingly honorable intentions, many parents have handicapped rather than advantaged their children. College has become a major "wake-up" for a generation of new freshmen, who have never received an "average" grade and rarely have been told that the results of their efforts are unsatisfactory.

In more than a few cases, this "make believe" world, where no less-than-positive feedback is furnished, continues after college matriculation. Such scenarios often do not prepare students for life after college, where there are high expectations, constant evaluation, and substantial consequences for substandard performance. When parents, teachers, or admissions officers collude (even unwittingly) in declaring the inadequate to be good and the mediocre to be excellent, we set our students up for failure, profound disappointment, and possibly permanent immaturity.

Included in Dr. Connell's book are realistic assessments of the problem, and more importantly, there are practical recommendations for addressing this increasingly pervasive problem. Reality may be the best way to prepare students for the real world. To do otherwise seems tantamount to telling someone that they can and will fly without having provided them with the skills and equipment needed to take flight, navigate, and return to the ground successfully. As discussed well in *Flying without a Helicopter,* our goal and guiding principle should be the development of persons to whom we would want to offer a job as well as have as a colleague. It is hard to see how the current practice will get us to that happy outcome.

—Jim Blackburn, EdD

Dr. Blackburn is retired and independently consults with campuses of the California State University as well as other institutions of higher education. His recent career consists of: Director of Admissions and Records at California State University, Fullerton, Director of Enrollment Management Services at the California State University Officer of the Chancellor, and Associate Vice President of Enrollment Services at California State University, Los Angeles.

PREFACE

Who Am I, and Why Did I Write This Book?

Fast-forwarding through my life to where this book starts, here is my background in one paragraph. I grew up in Cambridge, Massachusetts; went to Harvard and studied electrical engineering; moved out to Silicon Valley; and worked as an engineer for eight years. During that time, I traveled extensively and realized I was more interested in solving people problems than electrical ones. I went back to school and got a PhD in psychology from the University of California, Berkeley. In the middle of that transition, I lived in Europe for two years, married an American, and moved back to San Francisco with him. When we were ready to start a family, we moved to San Diego to enjoy the good life of shorter commutes, more affordable housing, and fantastic weather. Since then, I have been working as an organizational consultant, professor, and career coach. The book starts after we had a child and sent her off to school.

When my daughter was nearly three, I was looking forward to her starting preschool for several reasons. One was that I was hoping to meet some other parents and make some friends in San Diego. With that in mind, I volunteered to help the Parents Association on several projects, and two things immediately struck me: First, the "parents" consisted solely of moms. In fact, the generic term for any parent at the school was "mom": room mom, lunch mom, field trip mom, and so on. I wondered if I had, for the second time, jetted back to the 1950s. Where were all the dads? Oh, working. Second, the moms had a feistier schoolyard competition than their children. It was truly like being in high school again (and my daughter was only in preschool!). Helping out was the wrong approach to making friends. Rather, it made enemies. Once it became clear that I had any competence, I was seen as a threat that had to be squelched. The "popular" moms dressed in Prada and hung out in cliques, blocking the entrance to the school so you had to inch by them as you said "Good morning" and were ignored in response. The powerful moms ran the show—chaired the annual gala, hosted the annual wine donation fete, bullied volunteers in the hot lunch program, and bought their way onto the school board. The working moms were nowhere to be seen; they were out of the picture entirely.

But I digress. The competition was, on the surface, about the children. The real battle, however, was going on among the moms themselves. The children were merely the pawns. In this game, the goal was to have the best child. This was bigger than having the best child at any given moment (e.g., the star on the team or the highest scorer on a test). The goal was to have each child be the best at everything and build the best résumé so she or he would get accepted to the best college, which, presumably, would set them up to achieve the most success in life, reflecting the success of the driving force: the mom.

I had no idea résumés were already well underway for my daughter's kindergarten classmates. I thought that résumés started when you graduated from college and were looking for your first "real" job. But no, résumés had changed a great deal. They now included swimming lessons, toddler-level soccer teams, "outstanding artist" awards that everyone in the class received, and so on. I was years delinquent in constructing my daughter's résumé. After some initial panic, I screwed my head back on and told myself I refused to write a résumé for a kid in school. And I didn't—until she was eight and wanted to try out for a play and I was forced (against my policy) to create a résumé noting her acting experience. I did the writing, because my eight-year-old had no idea how to make an acting résumé and no clue what relevant experience she had.

I learned quickly that to construct great résumés, you must have your kids enrolled in dozens of extracurricular activities—and not just any extracurricular activities. They have to be desirable ones offered by highly respected (aka expensive) professionals. It requires parents (aka moms) to schedule, drive, and outfit their children in a manner that requires countless phone calls, trips to specialty stores and the bank, hours of negotiating with your children to go to these events, and hours of sitting around watching your children participate in the activities while competing with the other moms in the lobby. You can see why the minivan has become so popular. It serves as a recreation room during drives between activities, a changing room, a dining room, and a bedroom for drives during naptime or late at night.

The extracurricular activities are just a part of success building. Your child also has to be academically talented and the most popular student in the class. This often requires moms to hire specialists in math, reading, language, and so on to tutor their children and give them extra homework to do in between extracurricular activities. In addition, moms take control of their children's academic success by being in constant contact with their teachers and school principals and patrolling their children's homework (often doing it for them). They ensure their children's popularity by bringing cupcakes into class, having elaborate birthday parties with professional entertainers, and networking with the moms to make sure invitations to the right events are received.

Back to our story. I can't tell you how crazed I was to learn that my daughter had homework starting in kindergarten. I was a maniac at home, ranting and raving about how stupid it was to give five- and six-year-olds homework. I was so angry that the teachers invaded our home time by giving these young children busywork. Then, I found out I was supposed to monitor my daughter's "studies" and sign a form every day noting I had read to her for at least twenty minutes. I hit the roof. I hadn't been in school for a very long time, and I had absolutely no interest in reporting to a teacher now. Plus, I couldn't understand why the schools were encouraging parents to take control of their children's homework. I refused to be tricked into becoming a helicopter parent. I signed the papers when they were due but not because I had monitored her progress. That was up to my daughter.

It was also up to her to get me to sign the forms. If she didn't ask me for a signature, it didn't get done. I had to teach her some form of responsibility, after all. (You may think I was nuts to do that to a five-year-old, but believe me, they are up to the task.)

It was not just the teachers with whom I was at odds. I quickly found I was going against the grain of the other moms at school too, all of whom were playing the game. While I abhorred being required to sign my child's homework, the other moms made daily projects of reading the homework assignments, helping their children complete them, and making sure they were good enough to turn in (i.e., perfect). Fellow moms would meet for coffee and brag to each other about how good their (aka their child's) latest project was. They would say things like "We did this" or "I did that," barely making note of their child's involvement. In the fourth grade in California, children learn about California history. It is common for fourth graders to have to build a model of a Californian mission as a homework project. When my daughter was in fourth grade, they did not do that. I asked the teacher why, and he said they used to give that assignment until one child showed up with a professionally designed model that would have cost thousands of dollars to commission. (The kid's dad was an architect.)

My daughter had a project in the third grade on the American pioneers. The teacher sent a note home telling parents not to work on the projects; it should be the kids' work. I complied. I watched as my daughter showed me her completed abstract model of a wagon and an airplane, comparing the old and the modern methods of transportation. It was made completely of recycled materials—pieces of cardboard cut into the shapes of horses, a tissue covering the cardboard wagon with cardboard struts. I thought it was very creative. She got the equivalent of a "D" on the project because it wasn't snazzy enough. I swung by the classroom to have a glimpse of the other projects and found models with store-bought figurines and trees laid out on plaques with painted clay buildings. Clearly the parents had helped, and those were the projects that were praised. We were totally against the grain.

As I complained bitterly that the young children had so much homework, my fellow moms were asking the teachers to increase the homework or at least give them special homework so their children could excel. They stressed out if their children got less than a perfect score on their math or reading assessments. They hired tutors, sent their kids to after-school classes, and had special meetings with their teachers. I didn't understand the anxiety. I had always learned that some kids do better than others in math and reading, kids learn at different paces, some kids are superstars at sports, some are great musicians, and that is all fine. My fellow moms felt their children had to be superstars at math and reading and sports and music and whatever else there was. I felt so disconnected with the modern mom. I couldn't get myself worked into a tizzy over grades or which high school my daughter would get into. I just wanted her to be challenged, get a well-rounded education, build character, and make friends. I would tell fellow moms to chill out, but my advice fell on deaf ears.

I realized that I was, in effect, a pioneer. Baby boomer moms and Gen X cuspers (first members of a generation) who unknowingly followed in the boomers' footsteps surrounded me. I didn't understand their values and their approaches to parenting. I kept telling myself that a backlash to all this pressure had to be on the horizon. What I didn't realize at the time was that we had to wait for a sufficient segment of the next generation to push back. That is what is beginning to happen now. There are several movements, for example, to reduce the amount of homework for children. "The Race to Nowhere" movement is one of them, with a movie of the same title that is being shown to parents around the nation to help them realize the pressures their children are under and what negative effects this can cause, including suicide.

Perhaps it's my engineering brain that needs to know how things work, or maybe it's my psychologically minded self that must know what drives people. Ever since I saw parents behaving completely differently from the generation of their parents, I have been curious as to how that could happen. Generations typically differ from each other in certain ways, but they tend to be more similar than different overall. For example, baby boomers went through their hippie phase, when older people thought they were slackers and had no motivation to work. That changed quickly as they became yuppies. Gen Xers suffered from the same reputation when they were in their twenties, and now they are working hard to make ends meet. Millennials (Generation Y) are also getting a bad reputation in the workplace as they embark on their careers. It will be interesting to see what happens to them over the next decade or two. At the same time, today's parents are markedly different from yesterday's parents. They are more coddling, more competitive, more anxious, and more frenetic than ever before. Why is this? And how is this affecting the way these kids behave and cope as adults, at work, at home, and in life?

As a cusper, I was often unwittingly leading the causes of my generation. I infiltrated a man's profession, strove for equality, sought work-life balance, and explored the challenges and opportunities of working virtually before they were common issues among Gen X. I talked vigorously about these issues and tried to get support for my viewpoints, but I was going against the grain every step of the way. By the time people were ready to hear my messages, I had moved on to something else. Not this time. I know many people aren't ready to hear this message, but I have to put it out there anyway. The time will come when these questions will be central to my generation's thinking.

ACKNOWLEDGMENTS

I'd like to acknowledge all of the people who made the book a better product. Adrienne Moch edited the first copy of the manuscript. Traci Anderson and the anonymous reviewer in the Editorial Evaluations Department at iUniverse gave numerous tips on how to make the manuscript suitable for publication. In addition, I found the entire iUniverse team to be extremely skilled and professional.

Two editors at Berrett-Koehler, Neal Maillet and Anna Leinberger, were exceptionally helpful. In addition to providing the exact feedback I needed to successfully publish, they were personally supportive through the publication process. I am also grateful to the entire Berrett-Koehler staff and community. They are comprised of special individuals who are caring and generous and who truly make the world a better place.

I'd like to thank Maia Maltas for creating the images for this book, including the cover image. Maia took the risk of drawing cartoons for my book when I asked her to. It was not an easy task, because it was her first time doing it, despite the fact that she is obviously quite talented. She persevered even though she found the task "tortuous" at times and had to render many drafts until she satisfied her aesthetic eye. She is a role model of risk taking and resilience for us all.

My marketing team consisted of both professionals at Weaving Influence and dear friends. Together, Weaving Influence team members Becky Robinson, Ashleigh Tweedie, Max Stone, and Carrie Koens, and friends Diane Boudreau Yanofsky, Eric Roth, and John Thornburgh helped me identify my primary audience and focus my message. They all offered remarkable insights and support. Megan Constantino was also a key contributor to my marketing efforts. As I learned early on in the publication process, writing is only a small part of publishing a book. Without marketing, a book is just a message without reach.

Two mentors were particularly supportive with the publication process: Bernardo Ferdman and Julie O'Mara. They are what Bill Treasurer calls "open door leaders." They know that, to be a great leader, you need to open doors for others. They both helped me in this way, and they have inspired me to open doors for others too.

Friends and family have been invaluably helpful and supportive. They have kept me on track by pointing out resources and examples both for and against my messages. Sarah Block was particularly supportive in this regard, as well as in reconfiguring my website. I welcome the continued support and dialogue from thoughtful people. It is my goal to create an ongoing discussion about how best to prepare people for work and life.

INTRODUCTION

What Is This Book About?

This book is about what it takes to be successful in the workplace and how to get there. It is about parenting, educating, and managing to help kids and young adults build the skills and inner strength to succeed in an increasingly competitive world. It advises parents, educators, and managers on what is important to help produce healthy, independent, self-reliant employees who will thrive on their own instead of running home to Mommy and Daddy for support and protection. This book is also written for young adults. In fact, there are recommendations written directly to young adults in each chapter in Part 2.

The advice in this book is based on decades of experience in working and consulting with employees, managers, and executives in the business world. It is based on my expertise on what it takes to make it in the real world of work accumulated over twenty years of experience in the workplace and over a decade of research in academic literature and the media. It is also based on a collection of exclusive interviews with leaders and employees in the workplace.

How to Read This Book

This book is written for parents, educators, managers, and youth. It doesn't have to be read cover to cover. Rather, you may find it useful to go straight to the chapter(s) that interest you. However, the book does follow a logical sequence that builds upon previous chapters. To better understand the solutions, it is worth first understanding the problems.

Of course, some of you—you know who you are—will not have the patience to read through that and you will want to jump straight to the solutions. Feel free. Check out the exercises at the end too.

Part 1 outlines the problems young people are facing in the workplace and what it generally takes to succeed at a job. Chapter 1 is written from the manager's perspective. It describes the frustrations managers are currently experiencing in trying to get young employees to perform up to expectations. Several key areas are identified that are addressed in more detail in Part 2. Chapter 2 describes what real life is like at work and what it takes to succeed in that environment. Decades of research support the competencies that are identified as critical for success.

Each chapter in Part 2 deals with a particular subject area, including perfectionism, independence, resilience, interpersonal communication, and creativity. These chapters give specific advice in the form of research findings, case examples, reflection exercises, and actions to put into practice that are designed to help both parents and youth build their skills in these areas.

Part 3 contains exercises for each chapter in the book. The exercises appear in two forms: reflection questions and action tasks. The intention of this book is to get people to question their assumptions and behaviors and think about how they want to behave moving forward. The reflection questions raise issues for discussion and thinking, while the action tasks help you take steps to change your behavior if you so choose.

PART 1
Problems

CHAPTER 1

What Is Going On at Work?

As a child: "Mom, throw this away for me."

As an adult: "Mom, can you call my boss and tell him I don't understand this?"

A few years back, I gave a talk to a law firm about generational differences in work styles. The meeting consisted of lawyers at all levels. Because it was the summer, the law school student interns were invited to watch. I was in the process of going over differences of work styles between baby boomers, Generation Xers, and millennials, when a senior partner (a baby boomer) suddenly shot up from his chair and went on a diatribe about how lazy millennial workers are and how they should not be hired at all within the firm. Needless to say, he got people's attention. The younger associates immediately jumped up and fought back. They were lawyers, so they fought with words, not fists, but it got so heated I began to worry that a brawl wasn't out of the question. The interns looked on from the sidelines, wide-eyed. I had to jump in to defuse the situation. It was one of the more memorable seminars of my career.

In a completely different industry, another executive recently said one of her company's biggest problems with newly hired young workers is that they aren't able to work with others. She said they lack communication skills, something that is interesting because the millennial generation is known for liking to work in collaborative groups. However, in this executive's experience (which is not atypical), teamwork had not gone as smoothly as she would have liked with the new generation of employees.

In a similar vein, the CEO of a large technology company said he has had bad experiences with millennial generation employees. In his experience, the millennials whom they employed did not get the work done, were not willing to put in the time and effort to get the results the company was looking for, and were difficult to work with. He said he encouraged people at his company not to hire anyone less than thirty years old. This may be the new ageism.

A director at a health services provider complained about parents of her employees getting involved at work. She said when she turned down a job applicant, his mother called. Parental involvement at work is a common occurrence today. The *New York Times* reported on a survey conducted in 2006 by the career website Experience, Inc. Of the four hundred respondents, 25 percent said their parents were involved in their jobs "to the point that it was either annoying or embarrassing" (Belkin 2007). Examples include calling the boss to get time off on holidays, negotiating salaries, and asking for promotions for their adult children. Managers are put off by having to talk to their employees' parents, and they are becoming concerned that their employees are incapable of taking care of themselves.

These examples are prototypical of what is happening in the workplace today. Numerous articles have been published that depict the differences between older and younger workers. For example, The Conference Board is an internationally renowned association that supports organizations and provides best-practice research to for-profit and not-for-profit organizations. One of their recent executive action white papers is titled "Will you want to hire your own kids? (Will anybody else?)." The paper features comments from CEOs of several major corporations that focus on how recent graduates are lacking the skills needed for the workplace ("Will you want to hire your own kids? [Will anybody else?]" 2009).

The Millennial Generation

As much as parents oversend the message to their millennial children that they are special, there is no denying that the millennial generation is special in some ways. They are the most tech savvy, most educated, and most prepared generation of all time. That said, they have some critical blind spots that could lead to quick derailment once they are in the workplace. Their preparation for the future is coached, taught, protected, and academically shielded from the real world. This is the crux of what this book is about. My goal is to shift our approach to preparing children for the future from a narrow, academic approach to a well-rounded one. Academics are important, but life is much broader than that.

Countless books and articles have been written on the characteristics of the millennial generation. In addition to their bountiful education and technical skills, research has shown that millennials, as compared to previous generations, tend to want to be more collaborative, are accustomed to working in teams, and have a passion for pressure (Shih and Allen 2007). They change jobs frequently, want lifelong learning, expect on-the-job training, and want to proactively plan their own careers (Kim, Knight, and Crutsinger 2009; Meister 2012; Westerman and Yamamura 2007; Zemke, Raines, and Filipczak 2000). They are motivated by different factors from previous generations (such as advancement potential and free time) more than money or greater responsibilities, per se (Barford and Hester 2011). What really matters to them is getting what they want on a personal level (Fisher 2009). The post-millennial generation wants this even more.

Specific Trends in the Workplace

Early Career Burnout

Twenty-somethings are experiencing work stress and burnout at disturbingly high rates (Jager-Hyman 2009; Khidekel 2010; "Stress in America Findings" 2010). Previously, career burnout was a midlife issue. Now it is happening early on, at the beginning of people's careers. The twenty-somethings are showing signs of burnout by asking for time off or reduced work hours, or are opting out altogether and moving back with their parents. There is also a trend for young people to start their own companies that have more relaxed work schedules. Other signs include the increased use of prescription drugs and alternative relaxation methods, such as yoga and acupuncture, among young workers.

A recent survey by The Conference Board found that 64 percent of workers under twenty-five were unsatisfied with their jobs, versus just 44 percent in 1987 (and still higher than any other demographic in the workforce; Khidekel 2010).

Twenty-something millennial women are particularly at risk of career burnout. They report higher stress levels in numerous studies around the world. Similar to millennial men, they have worked so hard to get to the light at the end of the education tunnel only to find they are merely at the beginning of the career tunnel. They see a dubious future and want to get out but are strapped down with colossal student loans. Unlike men, it seems modern women have been so intent on asserting their independence that they are not as apt to take care of themselves when they are stressed. Some may rather work themselves into the ground than cut back to balance their lives or depend on a husband for support. In any case, they are more stressed and burned out than their male counterparts (Faw 2011).

Many millennial women didn't think of their lives beyond landing the initial first job. "They need to learn life is a marathon, not a sprint," says Kelly Cutrone, president of People's Revolution PR and author of *If You Have to Cry, Go Outside: And Other Things Your Mother Never Told You.* It's not as if these women expected their jobs to be parties and good times, but many underestimated the actual day-to-day drudgery (Faw 2011).

Millennial men and women alike seem to have higher expectations of work satisfaction than people of previous generations. A recent study of early career burnout found that high work ideals, or high expectations, were a significant cause of early career burnout. High expectations that are not matched in real working life may cause a reality shock that increases the risk of burnout (Djordjevic 2010).

Why do millennials have such great expectations? Millennials seem to have a sense that they deserve the fast track without having to put in the effort. They expect to have interesting jobs that do not impinge on their personal lives. When they are stuck doing drone work, such as answering phones, they balk. "What I see as boredom, they see as burnout," says a thirty-year-old Gen X owner of a marketing firm (Khidekel 2010). The generations before have had to work their way up the ladder, often putting in long hours and sacrificing personal time to advance. Some may argue that millennials are too soft and entitled, and they cannot take the pressure. Others might say millennials have already put in the time and sacrifice at school and are now ready for the payoff. What's more, millennials have had terrible luck with their timing. They have worked insanely throughout school with the promised payoff of the dream job, and then the economic crisis hit. No wonder they are burned out and dissatisfied!

When all is said and done, the depressed economy may be adding challenges for young people, but it is not the root of the problem. Millennials have a reputation of impatience and dissatisfaction, jumping from job to job. For example, a supervisor at a call center said the turnover rate for twenty-somethings is *every two months.* Most companies have a ninety-day probationary period to see if the employee is working out. Over the years, companies have found it takes three months to settle into a new job and see if the employee can handle it. The millennials at the call center are quitting before they've even given it a fair chance.

Hand Holding

The impressions millennials are making on the people who are already in the workforce are not entirely positive. They appear self-confident and vulnerable at the same time. They seem to need constant feedback and support—and the feedback has to be positive, even glowing.

One doctor relayed his experiences of giving feedback to residents. He said the young residents are so accustomed to being told how wonderful they are that when he gives them negative evaluations, they leave his office in tears. The millennials aren't used to losing. They have been told repeatedly that "everyone's a winner," and they have been sheltered from defeat along the way. They are under the impression that they are amazing. Look at their résumés, after all. They need to keep this vision of themselves alive to maintain their self-esteem that has been artificially inflated by years of bogus praise.

In addition to praise, managers complain that younger workers need constant reassurance that they are on track. Managers complain they don't have time to give the up-to-the-minute feedback these employees seem to expect. The managers also say these workers aren't able to move forward with their tasks without instructions at every step of the way. They seem to have difficulty working independently and taking a project and running with it.

Advice for managers of engineers from *The Engineering Daily*:

"Based on some of the responses we received from a recent survey of Gen Y's, most of the respondents indicated that they constantly desire to know how they are doing; if they are performing the task fast enough and more importantly if they are performing the task correctly. In fact, some of the respondents indicated that they would not mind receiving feedback on a daily basis" (Fred 2010).

Managers comment on how "high maintenance" the young workers are. They also comment on the lack of creativity of the new generation of workers. They seem to expect to be told what to do (but not in an authoritative way) and how to do it, sometimes to the point of managers wondering if it would be simpler just to do the work themselves.

Not only are employees depending on more support from their managers and colleagues, but they also are depending on support from their parents at work. It is commonplace for adult workers to text or call their parents multiple times during the workday for support and advice. Managers are also complaining about having to take time to deal with their employees' parents. Parent calls range from simply informing the manager that the employee is sick to demanding a promotion for the employee. Managers and recruiters increasingly have to involve the parents in the hiring process, as well.

Examples of employers encouraging parent involvement at work:

- **In 2006, Merrill Lynch offered its first "parents day" for the parents of interns to tour the trading floor in downtown New York City and see what it is like to work there (Weiss 2006).**
- **The president of an engineering firm called a newly hired employee's mother and asked her to be there for her daughter's first day of work. He gave them both a tour of the facility (Hira 2007).**

Human resources departments in many Fortune 500 companies are now tasked with answering questions from the parents of job candidates. The parents also call to set up and manage interview schedules for their children. Many companies now have websites dedicated to parents, offering handbooks and other resources for them to evaluate potential employers for their grown children (Alsop 2008).

Lack of Communication and Relationship-Building Skills

"I couldn't believe it," says the veteran San Diego lifeguard. "A kid shouted, 'Hey, look!' and I saw two of them with their parents, and suddenly realized 'oh my God. On a day like today, when it was 80-some degrees outside—at Mission Bay!—that's the first voice I've heard all day.'" It never used to be that way, says the lifeguard, Rod Messinger. "Gradually, it's just gotten to the point where you don't hear kids anymore. I mean, it's just silent" (Manson 2009).

When talking with managers at organizations, often the first complaint they have about their younger employees is their lack of communication skills. Millennials are used to interacting with each other in short electronic chats and communicating in slang, abbreviations, and memes. Millennials are used to working at a fast pace and are used to getting immediate results. Immediacy is important to them; patience is not (Meister and Willyerd 2010). Neither are the skills of speaking and writing formally. In terms of writing, millennials have a tendency to rush through projects and turn in completed work without fine-tuning or proofreading. They copy and paste rather than write out things. I have heard countless complaints from managers of younger employees turning in work that is literally unusable.

In terms of interacting, millennials are accustomed to multitasking and working in a digital time frame, which does not offer much opportunity to reflect or control emotions. They respond quickly and impulsively, which can compromise teamwork. Millennials are known for being less empathic than other generations, meaning they do not feel what others feel. They are also known for being more narcissistic, meaning they focus more on themselves. Narcissists do not see their impact on others as well as non-narcissists. They criticize others and promote themselves. Narcissists are not good team players.

Ironically, millennials are known for being more collaborative; they like working in groups. It seems they would have great communication skills, but from what managers are saying, that is not the case. Impulsivity tends to create conflict in teams, and this is exactly what managers are complaining about now. Lack of self-control, especially in the form of emotional control, seems to be one of the major contributing factors to the communication problems at work.

Building relationships is another challenge for millennials because of their history of communicating virtually more than face-to-face. Research shows that virtual interactions contain less trust than face-to-face interactions. There is less rapport and more conflict and disagreement. People tend to feel freer to say what they want in virtual interactions. They aren't as diplomatic or respectful as in face-to-face meetings.

With the millennials' tendency to interact more often virtually than face-to-face, their relationships are more tenuous and less reliable. Millennials will tell you they are, in fact, closer to more friends than older people are. They feel they are connected to their friends because they share interests, ideas, and opinions with them. However, the distance of the screen creates a safety zone for them. They don't have to interact "live" or in the moment. They can compose a witty response on their keyboard and not be caught tongue-tied. They can ignore a message and not be on the spot to respond to it immediately.

More importantly, people have fewer obligations in virtual relationships. Yes, they can feel connected, but what do they owe each other? If someone is sick, will their Facebook friends go out and buy juice for them or take them to the doctor? (Or do they call their parents for this?) If someone has to duck out of the office for an hour on a personal errand, will their Twitter followers cover for them in front of the boss? (Are they colocated?) Are they willing to put their jobs on the line for their Instagram contacts? (And is that even a sacrifice if they can move back home?)

A Comfortable Environment

An employer's view of a good job candidate: a self-starter, focused, hardworking

A millennial's view of a good job: a fun atmosphere, great lattes, yoga classes at lunch

A senior partner at a law firm told me he was puzzled as to why his junior associates had to stop at Starbucks on the way to court. He was in a hurry to get there early to be ready to argue in front of the judge, whereas the associates were more concerned with getting no-foam lattes.

Gen X started the trend to have a more comfortable workplace. Perhaps this began as a reaction to having a less comfortable workplace, consisting of cubicles instead of offices. In any case, millennials have taken it to the next level. Work has to be comfortable, as well as fun, exciting, praiseworthy, and a growth experience. Companies are introducing new formats for work that include games to attract millennial workers. Really.

The millennials have been entering the workplace with unrealistic expectations. They don't realize they will have to work long hours and do work they consider drudgery. They are used to cushy, fun environments, listening to music on their iPods, and chatting with friends on Facebook, with moms, dads, coaches, and others poring over them to meet their needs and tell them how wonderful and special they are. They expect nothing less at work. The cliché of the millennials is they want a trophy for just showing up. (And why not? They have received trophies for that in the past.) They are accustomed to having a team of adults working to develop them and presume the managers and others at work are there to do just that. When they come face-to-face with the fact that the managers think *they* work for *them,* they think the managers just do not get it.

The clash between employer and employee expectations is resulting in some interesting trends. First, as this chapter has unsubtly implied, is that there is a generational divide in the workplace. There is often an "us versus them" attitude among the generations. The old think the young are lazy and entitled. The young think the old are incompetent and inefficient. There are many books and consultants to give organizations advice on how to reduce this conflict and work together more productively. I have given numerous workshops on this topic.

Second, the economic downturn has given the employers the upper hand. They can be more selective about whom they hire and fire. They can refuse to meet the demands of the workers, and the workers either have to "suck it up" or leave. Because the baby boomers and Gen Xers don't have such high expectations of the workplace, they are the ones who "suck it up" and the millennials are pushed out or they opt out on their own volition.

Third, the millennials don't tend to need their jobs as much as the older workers because their parents are willing to take care of them.

Therefore, they don't feel the need to work in substandard conditions. When the going gets tough, they move back home, and their parents shoulder the weight. Thus, they do not have the need for the job that employees historically have had. There is no stigma for quitting. They will not feel like failures. Rather, they will say their employer failed them.

Entitlement

A Harvard alumna used to volunteer to interview Harvard college applicants. She expressed that she stopped doing it because the applicants were so hard to schedule interviews with. She said they would tell her—their required Harvard interviewer—they were too busy to meet with her and they wanted her to work around their schedules. Some didn't even show up. Some parents returned the call for their kids and berated her for not being more flexible. She said that, in her opinion, she was very flexible. Her kids were older and she didn't work, so she could be flexible, but it wasn't enough for some parents and applicants.

Last, but far from least, is the hot topic of entitlement. It *never fails* to come up when I am talking to managers. I have innumerable stories about "entitled" workers. These stories tend to reflect the theme of "I'm ready for you to 'wow' me, to give me work tailored to my needs and interests, that I will find fun and exciting and will develop me for my career, work I deem worthy and won't take up too much of my time." There is a silent follow-up of "You owe me this, and I owe you nothing in return." These workers expect to get the exciting challenges right away. They think they know how to do it because they have "done it in school." They think if they have done something once, they have learned and perfected it and now it is time to move onto something different and more exciting. The attitude can be summed up by "what's in it for me?"

A director of training and development at a large healthcare provider shared a story about a twenty-four-year-old employee. The employee missed the deadline for applying for a scholarship and demanded to be able to apply anyway. When the person who took the scholarship applications said "no," she went to their boss. When the boss said "no," she went to their boss and kept up until she reached the director. The director also said "no" over the phone, but the woman insisted on meeting with her. The director said she'd talk to her to explain her decision. The twenty-four-year-old employee showed up to the meeting *with her mother* and insisted that she be able to apply for the scholarship. To the director's astonishment, the employee said she had missed the deadline because she was on vacation—and she still fully believed she should be allowed to apply. The director said "no," to both the employee and her mother.

One of the challenges of getting millennials to work hard at boring tasks is that they are not afraid to quit if they don't like what they are doing. Many millennials have never had jobs where they have had to work hard at boring tasks. Many have never had jobs at all. They have never had to work. Instead, they have spent summers going to specialized leadership programs and educational internships. The owner of a chain of bicycle stores said she (and other colleagues in retail) used to depend on hiring college students to work in their stores. Over the last several years, however, college students have stopped applying for these jobs. It is an unfortunate situation, because the stores are suffering from a lack of employees and the college students are suffering from a lack of work experience. It's ironic, when people are complaining they can't find jobs due to the depressed economy.

Yes, the millennial attitude of making work more about employees and less about employers is certainly a long-needed movement in the direction of humanizing the workplace. At the same time, there is a limit to how much the employers (and our society as a whole) will be willing to take this. France, for example, has a much more humane workplace in terms of hours worked, vacation, and health care. However, France is far from a business leader. If Americans want to stay at the top (or even toward the top) of the food chain, sacrifice and hard work will need to continue. It will be interesting to see, over the next decade, how this ambivalence plays out. Right now, however, hard work is still expected.

The Post-Millennial Generation

I don't mean to pick on millennials. They are just the first generation to widely exhibit certain critical blind spots. Parenting approaches that create these gaps are still in place and are going farther down the continuum of extremity. The next generation—yet to be named— is also at risk.

CHAPTER 2

What You Need at Work

The funny thing about college is how little of it applies to work. I remember thinking that when I had my first job after graduation. I was an electrical engineer. Yes, as an engineer I had to use my knowledge of circuitry to design data communications equipment. However, that was hardly enough. Real circuits had to be cost-effective, withstand temperature differences, adhere to international standards, and so on. Designing circuits was only a small part of the job. Also, politics makes or breaks you in the office. They don't teach you that in college.

Success Factors at Work

Fifty executives at a large pharmaceutical company went through an assessment center to help the company develop its talent pipeline. They were assessed on sixteen competencies, or success factors. "Technical expertise" (what you learn in college) was just one factor; being socially agile, building strategic relationships, influencing others, maintaining composure under pressure, and driving change were among the fifteen other critical factors that are not taught in college.

Most medium- to large-sized companies have talent management systems consisting of sets of competencies for each job or job level against which employees are measured. Typically, employees are measured during annual or semiannual performance reviews. A good performance review will include a development plan so employees know which areas to develop to be better at their jobs and work toward promotion. Many companies develop custom competency models for their employees and leaders, but they generally have several factors in common. Table 1 lists success factors often used in the workplace to evaluate job performance. These competencies are written for organization leaders, but you can easily see how many of them apply to people on all levels, in some form or another.

Table 1: Common Success Factors at Work (for Leaders)

Success Factor	Description
Leadership, courage, and decision-making ability	Gravitates toward leadership positions, is not afraid to make tough decisions, and can make good-quality decisions quickly
Social agility, being a team player, and building relationships	Is emotionally intelligent, works well with others, has people skills, and makes strategic alliances
Building teams and developing others	Identifies talent, brings the right mix of people on board, manages low performers, and creates an environment where people learn and develop their skills
Communication and influence	Is able to articulate verbally and in writing, influences others, and listens
Cognitive ability and analytical thinking	Is smart, has the ability to think strategically and tactically and focus on what is necessary at the time
Creativity, innovation, and entrepreneurialism	Develops creative solutions to problems; creates new ideas, processes, and products; fosters creativity in others
Planning and execution	Is organized, develops and follows processes to complete tasks, and holds others accountable for completing tasks as well
Facilitating and adapting to change; resilience	Generates positive change in the organization, adapts well to a rapidly changing environment, and stays strong in the face of failure

Success Factor	Description
Drive for results	Drives self and others to achieve outstanding results
Business acumen	Knows finance, marketing, operations, risk management, and other business concepts
Customer service orientation	Puts the customer first—both internal and external customers
Self-awareness and self-development	Is in touch with self, knows strengths and weaknesses, strives to develop self, and is a lifelong learner
Integrity and organizational values	Is honest, does the right thing, and takes on the organization's values as his/her own

No one is good at all of these. We all have some shortcomings, and we all have strengths that will lead us in one direction, as opposed to another. For example, a person who is very strong at business acumen—say, finance—but is not as strong at customer service would likely be more successful in the role of an accountant than in the role of a salesperson. That said, it is interesting to note how broad these success factors are. Technical expertise is only a tiny portion of what it takes to be a successful employee and, particularly, a successful leader. In other words, there is only so much that academic training can do for you to prepare you for being good at your job. You need much more than that.

Job Fit

One day, I was called in to give feedback to a company's leaders on one of their directors who had been through our assessment center. The meeting was curious to begin with, since exceptionally high-level people were there. The meeting was called unexpectedly after being put off for months after the completion of the assessment center program. But, being a consultant, I was used to flexing to the whims of clients. Within minutes, it was clear the meeting was not a typical collaborative evaluation of an executive, with people from inside and outside of the company bringing their observations to the table. It was a meeting to develop a case to fire the director for not being able to manage the relationships in a business alliance under his charge. The director was a smart, talented technical expert. He was not, however, skilled at building rapport and managing conflict. In the field, we call this a "derailing" factor. In other words, he was derailed from his upwardly mobile track because he did not have people skills. This is, unfortunately, a very common occurrence in organizations. It would have been better for the director if he had learned people skills or, even better, taken a job that better leveraged his technical skills.

I coached another mismatched director—a very smart and talented woman who was an extreme introvert. An introvert is someone who likes to be alone, who is not comfortable interacting with people. You can only imagine how absolutely miserable this woman was, when her job was to manage personal relationships among her team, her peers, and the board. She was desperate to change jobs without burning any bridges in the process. Unfortunately, this is also a common occurrence, especially in technology-based companies. Some introverts can develop quite good people skills. However, no introverts truly like it. Sometimes it is not about competence, but it is about job fit.

Job fit is important at all levels in an organization—manager, employee, consultant, business owner, and so on. One thing they do not teach you in college is what you will actually be *doing* in a career of your choosing. College students choose "majors," fields of study that hopefully hold their interest and in which they get good grades. (Many times majors are chosen because parents tell their children they need to be a doctor or lawyer to make the family proud.) Of equal or greater importance are the work environment and tasks associated with a particular job. For example, I had planned to be a therapist before I applied to graduate school in psychology.

Fortunately, I followed Richard Nelson Bolles's advice in *What Color Is Your Parachute?* (Bolles 1990). I conducted several informational interviews of people in the field before I applied. I asked what a typical day was like. One therapist told me it was a very passive job. You sit in a room all day long and listen to people as they come to you. I thought about that and realized I would hate that job. I needed to get outside, move around, and interact with people. I was so glad I had gotten that insight before wasting years and years of graduate education, internships, and eventual job experience before realizing I was in the wrong place. (I had already done that in my previous career as an engineer!)

> **"Indeed, it was the assembly line that inspired the industrial age school design, with the aim of producing a uniform, standardized product as efficiently as possible. Though the need to encourage thoughtful, knowledgeable, compassionate global citizens in the twenty-first century differs profoundly from the need to train factory workers in the nineteenth century, the industrial age school continues to expand, largely unaffected by the realities within which children are growing up in the present day" (Senge et al. 2004).**

Schools are beginning to change, albeit slowly. In response to businesses berating educational institutions on how impractical they are, colleges and lower schools are getting savvier about what is required in the workplace. Many curricula have been modified to add more real-world components, such as teamwork, presentation skills, and ethics. The college and graduate courses in the business school where I teach often require teamwork. Engineering students build robots in teams and compete against each other in tournaments. Kids in elementary school make PowerPoint presentations in front of the class. It is still just a beginning. And, frankly, schools may not be able to offer training in all the areas needed to be successful in the workplace. Nor should they. We have this other thing called "life" that is a great training ground for adulthood.

But I digress. We are talking about job fit, not skills and abilities. The point is people are much happier and more successful when they are in jobs that fit their personality and work style. It is not only about what they are good at. People thrive when they are in an environment that supports them rather than hinders them. Knowing what environments are a good fit requires a person to know about themselves—in other words, to have self-awareness. Effective people need to be self-aware for a number of reasons. Being in touch with your strengths and weaknesses, as well as what motivates you, will help you be more successful in your job (Tjan 2012).

Real Life at Work

We learn as babies that you can't always get what you want and temper tantrums do not usually achieve what you are looking for. We learn on the playground that you have to share and take turns to make friends. We learn from long car rides that your imagination can turn a dull time into an extraordinary one. We learn from heckling and teasing how to be tough, have a sense of humor, or fight back. We learn from games how to lose gracefully. Have you ever watched a child learn how to jump rope or shoot a hoop? Have you seen how much perseverance children can have to make it to ten skips or get a single basket? They may scream out in frustration, slam down the ball, or cry in the process, but they'll get back up and keep going until they get it—that is, of course, if a parent doesn't intervene to make them "feel better."

Step back for a moment and think about what life is really like in the workplace. It is rarely fun and rewarding. (But, hopefully, it sometimes is!) Work involves a lot of drudgery and effort and lots of frustration. It's why we get paid to do it. Table 2 lists things we often encounter at work.

Table 2: Things We Encounter at Work

Things We Encounter at Work	Examples
Boredom	The lull between the lunch and dinner rushes or after a big project is complete, when you don't have enough to do, or when the work is unfulfilling
Tedious work	Filling out timesheets, proofreading, checking and rechecking the math to make sure it is correct, teaching the same course over and over again, washing the dishes, dealing with the same cranky customers day after day, or working on the same station on the assembly line year after year
Problems	The photocopier is jammed and you need the copies ten minutes ago; your key scientist quits in the middle of the experiment; your competitor just released the product your company has been working on and was counting on for revenue; the supplier is out of the product you need; the power goes down; your kid is sick and you have no child care on the day of an important presentation
Barriers	Your coworker won't share the information you need to complete your part of the project; no one is planning to retire anytime soon so you won't have any opportunities for promotion; your spouse just got transferred to the Bangladesh facility; the meeting is in Tokyo and you're afraid of flying
"No."	You ask your boss for more time to complete your project and she says "no"; you ask for the day off to go to your sister's wedding and your boss says "no"—no, you can't wear jeans to work, you can't have the project you want, you can't add another team member to lighten the workload, you can't come to the meeting to present the project you completed, and you can't work from home even if you get more done there

Things We Encounter at Work	Examples
Mistakes	Your recently released code has a bug in it; the car needs to be recalled because of a safety problem your team was in charge of; you got the facts wrong in an article that has already gone to print; you shoot a guy you thought was pulling out a gun but it was really a cell phone; you ordered one thousand crates of eggs instead of eggplants
Failures	You lose the account; you get fired; the patient dies on the operating table; the company stock plunges after the acquisition you authorized; your medicine doesn't get FDA approval; you need to close the restaurant because you can't pay the bills; you lose the election and now you have to make the concession speech to your supporters
People	People with more experience than us or less experience than us, smart people, not-so-smart people, difficult people, mean people, emotional people, people with different interests and values, and bullies
Teamwork	You don't get along with all your teammates; someone isn't carrying his load; someone doesn't know what she's doing; someone isn't communicating with the team; the team leader has favorites and you're not one of them
Insufficient resources	There is no administrative support, so you have to do it all yourself; there is no paper in the photocopier, and you won't be getting any more until next week; you can't pay overtime but need the team to work extra hours anyway; there aren't enough buses to get all the kids to school
Ethical dilemmas	The boss wants you to use the cheaper building material for the school, but it's not as structurally sound; you see your coworker taking drugs at work (do you tell, and what if he's a taxi driver?); you are extremely attracted to your hot, married employee who keeps coming on to you; there are discriminatory hiring practices at your company; you've got a spectacular story for the paper, but you know your source is unreliable

Things We Encounter at Work	Examples
Ambiguity	Your boss travels 75 percent of the time, and you aren't sure exactly what you are supposed to be doing; you're told to "do whatever it takes" to make the numbers add up—is this my job or yours?
Competition	There are six associate lawyers, and there is only one partnership opening; there is only one salesperson of the year; you've made it into the top round of interviews; your colleague wants your job
High stakes	Your client faces the death penalty; the bank is threatening foreclosure if you don't make the next payment on time; the merger will force ten thousand workers out of a job
Change	Your entire product line has been canceled, and you need to find something else to do at the company or you'll be out of a job; the company has been bought out, and your department is being moved to Atlanta; we are moving toward a more centralized system so you will no longer report to your current boss—you will be reporting to headquarters; we no longer allow telecommuting, so you must come into the office five days a week
Indifference, apathy	"Everyone knows we could process patients in half the time but no one cares to fix it." "We're comfortable with the way things are." "I'm just here to do my job." "It's good enough the way it is. Don't rock the boat."
Politics	You get transferred to an office forty-five minutes away to prosecute prison cases because you supported the DA who didn't win; you're being sidelined because you didn't stroke the boss's ego enough; you stay out too late to get a good night's sleep, drink the variety of shots your boss orders for the table, force yourself not to puke, and stagger several miles home because you're too drunk to drive, all to stay in the in-group

Things We Encounter at Work	Examples
Rules, laws	We need FDA approval to launch the drug; you must follow the Sarbanes–Oxley Act and personally oversee financial audits for your company; no piercings allowed; lunch must be taken from noon to twelve thirty; coffee must be served with a lid even if the customer doesn't want it
Lack of control	The company is bought out, and you may or may not end up with a job; you take a position with a wonderful boss, and a week later he is replaced with a horror of a boss; you have so many ideas for improvement, but they fall on deaf ears; the IT department replaces the software you know with a new program that is impossible to use; you get your work schedule for the week the night before

Wow! Work doesn't sound like so much fun after all, does it? Exactly. Life is often not so much fun either. There's a lot of drudgery involved to get by day to day. Life is not always delicious. Sometimes you just have to eat because you are hungry. We can't eat only desserts. (Yes, many of us wish we could, but unfortunately our bodies can't survive on sugar alone.) We have to eat the vegetables and proteins to build our strength and resilience to fight off disease and stay mobile. Mentally, it's the same thing. With the ups come the downs, and we need to be strong enough to get through the down times.

Life is not always delicious.

What exactly does it take to be successful in life? As much as we'd all like the quick fix—like the diet where you can eat anything or the exercise routine where you don't have to sweat—the formula really is about building strength and resilience to do the right thing and be true to yourself. I call the formula "REAL Life." It's "REAL" because it's real, and it's "REAL" because it's an acronym for Resilient-Empowered-Authentic-Limber. To succeed in real life, it's necessary to have these four characteristics.

REAL Life

Resilient
Empowered
Authentic
Limber

- **Resilient** is to stay engaged and maintain a positive attitude no matter what gets in your way.
- **E**mpowered is to be liberated, **independent**, confident, and able to get things done.
- **A**uthentic is to be aware of yourself, know your strengths and your **imperfections**, and **communicate** genuinely and transparently.
- **L**imber is to be flexible in mind and body, **creative**, resourceful, and able to switch gears quickly and seamlessly, as the situation requires.

It takes a lot to be successful in REAL life. REAL life is not easy. But we all have to start somewhere, and I have mapped the characteristics of people who succeed in REAL life to five actions (or solutions) you can take to achieve success in *your* REAL life. I emphasize *your* REAL life, because every life is different and success means different things to different people. Success in REAL life means achieving success in the way *you* define it for *you*. No matter how you define success, you will need to be resilient, empowered, authentic, and limber to get there. The five actions outlined in Table 3, below, will help you be REAL. Part 2 of the book goes through each of these actions in detail, chapter by chapter.

Table 3: REAL Life Actions for Success

Resilient **E**mpowered **A**uthentic **L**imber		**REAL Life Actions for Success**
Accept imperfection	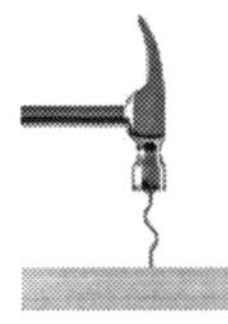	Praise less and appreciate imperfections in yourself and others.
Build resilience		Take risks, make mistakes, and learn from them, while retaining positive energy.
Develop independence		Make your own decisions and accept the consequences, take care of yourself, and initiate action.
Polish communication skills		Listen actively, be present in the moment, manage your emotions, and be authentic when interacting with others.
Foster creativity		Take time to reflect, let ideas flow on their own schedule, and let yourself have numerous bad ideas (failures) to inspire the good ones (successes).

PART 2
Solutions

An excerpt from the song “Numb” by Linkin Park (2003):

I’ve become so numb, I can’t feel you there
Become so tired, so much more aware
I’m becoming this, all I want to do
Is be more like me and be less like you.

CHAPTER 3
Accept Imperfection

There seems to be a movement toward having perfect children. In the past, parents felt they had done their job if their kids made it through childhood. Things like getting married, finishing high school, and getting a job were important. Going to college was great, if you were so lucky to have a kid who was bright enough to get in and want to go. As time went on, for the middle class, college gradually became a standard expectation. Now, it's not only expected that kids go to college, but also many of them are expected to go to graduate school too, and not any school will do.

It seems that kids today, unlike the rest of us, aren't allowed to have strengths and weaknesses. To get into a good college, they have to be "super people" (Atlas 2011). They have to be strong at everything. If they get 80s in math, they have tutors to raise their grades. They need to have the lead part in the school play, be an all-star athlete, win an award for writing the best essay, be the president of one club or another, have the best exhibit at the science fair, and, on top of it all, be popular. Wow, that's a lot of pressure!

Deresiewicz explains that the college admission standards have become so extreme that the kids who are accepted into elite colleges have only experienced success, never failure. "The prospect of *not* being successful terrifies them, disorients them. The cost of falling short, even temporarily, becomes not merely practical, but existential. The result is a violent aversion to risk. You have no margin for error, so you avoid the possibility that you will ever make an error" (Deresiewicz 2014).

How does this show up at work? To answer that, we need to take a step back for a moment. We need to ask ourselves if it is indeed possible to be a perfect person. Unless we have given birth to Leonardo da Vinci, the answer is probably not (and even he had flaws). Given that it is unlikely a person is strong at everything, it means they will have to work harder in some areas than others to be good at them. To be good at anything—really good, award-winning good—you have to work hard, even if you have natural talent. Lacking the natural talent makes it that much harder. Thus, to be great at everything will require an inordinate amount of work. For people who are naturally driven and gifted, this may be okay. They may not mind exhausting themselves to do what it takes to be great at several things (but no one can be great at everything).

People who are not naturally driven will want to find shortcuts. Even those who are driven and talented but are limited by the number of hours in a day may seek out shortcuts, which can include

- realizing your teacher does not read the homework, so you do a sloppy job or don't turn it in at all;
- cheating;
- taking drugs to give you extra energy;
- taking on leadership roles in clubs and not doing anything during your term;
- having your parents do the work for you;
- learning to talk your way into and out of anything; and
- believing you are perfect and blaming any mishaps on external forces, not your own.

Cheating

Lately, cheating has become rampant. Kids feel it is justified; they feel no remorse, not even when they get caught. For example, Nayeem Ahsan, a student at Stuyvesant High School in New York, was caught in a massive cheating incident on the Regents exams in 2012. He was sharing the answers on three different exams with 140 other students—and this wasn't the first time he cheated. He had been collaborating with other students on tests and homework for quite some time. He was interviewed after he got caught, was suspended from school, and was waiting to find out if he would be allowed back. He mentioned he wished he had been cleverer so he would not have gotten caught, he felt justified in cheating because the pressure was too great and the teachers were too lazy to check, and he thought he should be allowed back at school. As for punishment, he said he had learned his lesson and he shouldn't be punished further. He said, "The fact that I could have gotten kicked out, that changed my life" (Kolker 2012). He was shooting for a career in investment banking and wanted to expeditiously get back on track.

This is the kind of thinking that is entering the workplace—that cheating is justified and doesn't warrant punishment. For investment banking, this kind of thinking may have been going on for a long time, but it seems to be permeating the rest of society too and at young ages. More importantly, is this the kind of thinking we want to enter the workplace? Someone who gets caught for massive embezzlement and thinks he should be allowed to keep his job? We, as parents and adults, are fostering this kind of thinking and behavior in at least two important ways:

1. We are putting so much pressure on kids to be perfect.
2. We are going too easy on them when they get caught.

Nayeem got caught a lot earlier sharing the answers to homework on Facebook, but his teacher decided not to turn him in. Did he learn his lesson then? It seems the lesson he learned was to be more careful when cheating. Ultimately, however, the school did not agree he had learned the right lesson the second time around, and they kicked him out.

The Emperor's New Clothes

Denial among parents is rampant. I am constantly astonished at how perfect parents think their children are. A parent might be telling you how honest her child is as that same child is walking behind her, holding forbidden cookies stolen from the pantry. If the parent does admit to seeing the child with the cookies, she will find some way to explain it to you or tell the kid it is okay just this one time. Parents do not want to see that their child is doing something wrong. They don't want to hear about it either; if you say something negative about a friend's child, you will be lucky to keep the friend at all.

Kids are praised constantly (to boost their self-esteem) to the point that they think they are perfect too. If you give anything less than stellar feedback to people like this, they will either reject it entirely or collapse like a balloon that has a hole in it. They can't cope. This is extremely problematic in the workplace, where the truth will come out that they are not perfect.

Perfectionism at Work

There are two schools of thought on perfectionism at work. The first is: It must be perfect. Documents must be spell-checked and proofread, code must be debugged, equipment must be inspected, and so on. In some cases, perfectionism is without a doubt expected. For example, no one wants to die in a plane crash. If the president makes a gaffe, he is ridiculed for a long time. If the reel goes down in the movie theater, there is practically a revolution. Hospitals have backup generators to keep people alive in storms. There are many scenarios in which errors are not tolerated.

Early in my career, I did some mechanical drafting. I designed pieces of equipment for a stratospheric balloon that took measurements of ozone and other elements in the Earth's atmosphere. The first piece

I designed was a simple little box that was to hold some electronics. It came back from the machine shop with screw holes all up and down one side and no holes in the adjoining side. Everyone laughed and said I had designed "Swiss cheese." I had gotten a tiny detail wrong in the orientation of the drawing that caused the whole box to be unusable. In this case, getting the details right was extremely important.

"The Devil is in the details."

At the same time, perfectionists can impede progress in organizations. We talk about the executive losing sight of the forest among the trees. If you pay too much attention to getting every single detail right, you may never make it to your end goal. I have seen numerous examples of this, ranging from doctoral candidates who cannot finish their dissertations because they are so worried about getting it right and engineers who miss their deadlines because they are so worried about writing just the right subroutine to middle managers who spend so much time micromanaging their team members that they don't deliver the results the company needs.

This brings us to the second school of thought on perfectionism: Results trump the tiny details. For example, Microsoft releases Windows with bugs every time and offers patches to fix them later. If they had waited to reach perfection before releasing Windows, Apple would be the world standard. In today's fast-paced world of business, we don't often have time to sit and reflect on the details or check and recheck our work product to get to perfection. Technology has fostered an acceptance of imperfection. Fast-written e-mails fraught with typos and grammatically incorrect sentences have gotten us used to ignoring mistakes. Now I rarely see a professional PowerPoint presentation without errors in it. Books and newspapers even contain typographical errors.

"A good garden may have some weeds."
—Thomas Fuller, *Gnomologia*, 1732

Neither camp is right—at least not all the time. Put another way, in the world of business (and everywhere), we need to decide when we need to get it right and when "good enough" is better. And when it needs to be right, "good enough" will not do. This can be problematic to people who are used to getting A-pluses for less than perfect work. First, they don't understand the difference between "good enough" and perfect, and second, they can't take the criticism that their work isn't good enough.

The Illusion of Perfectionism versus the Reality of Imperfectionism

"The closest to perfection a person ever comes is when he fills out a job application form."
—Stanley J. Randall

I had a prototypical experience of the conflict over perfectionism a while back when I was running an executive assessment center. We brought in executive candidates and ran them through a series of tests and business simulations to determine what their strengths and gaps were for positions on the executive board. We had top-level people in from a large and influential organization, and we were under pressure to give them a high-quality experience. It was a customized assessment center, so we had to adjust to the client feedback as it came in. That meant we frequently had to make changes to our materials.

Unfortunately, every time we brought in a new group of executives to be assessed, there were errors in the materials that caused confusion for the participants and made us seem unprofessional. The interns were responsible for editing and producing the materials. After several occurrences of having to bear the embarrassment of the errors in front of the executives and subsequently give the interns corrections, I expressed my frustration over the lack of quality in the work product. The interns looked at me like I was crazy. They couldn't believe I would get upset over a few errors. They clearly thought I was being one of those annoying perfectionists (old-school, mind you). I thought there was no excuse for producing unprofessional work. After all, how hard was it to proofread the documents? I could do it in a matter of minutes. Why couldn't they? Or, more precisely, why *wouldn't* they? Had they really gotten perfect scores at school by turning in work that contained errors?

I don't know ultimately how much our lack of quality mattered on this project. We finished a round of assessment centers for this client but were not hired back for more. Financial reasons were given for their decision. Another thing happened though. The interns did not like me anymore because I had criticized them. You could see that they were bruised from the perceived attack on their work, even though it was only the mildest of criticism by workplace standards. They did not bounce back or value the feedback. Rather, they tried to work with other people who only gave them positive feedback.

One more noteworthy thing happened on this project. The interns were frustrated that they had to keep doing the boring background work and were not given the opportunity to work directly with the executive candidates. Although I understood their desire to do the frontline work, I was surprised they thought they were ready. After all, they had not yet gotten the materials right. Didn't they need more practice at that first? Again, they looked at me like I was crazy. They said they knew how to develop the materials already, because they had already done it. They had no concept of practicing something until you get it right. Furthermore, they thought they should be able to work directly with the heads of a large company despite having had no practice at assessment. There was no concept of working up to it. They thought their schooling had given them everything they needed to give powerful executives feedback they could not even take themselves.

There are a number of issues at work in this case. The first was that there was a level of professionalism expected of the interns, and it was not being met. Second, there was a sense from the interns that they were perfect and able to do high-quality work without proving themselves. I fault the adults who had been giving them false feedback all along and telling them they were perfect even though they were not. As challenging as it was to deal with interns with such inflated egos, the situation was not their fault. They had been told repeatedly that they were perfect. They got A's in school (which are perfect grades) and were undoubtedly brought up with a great deal of praise at home too. They were certainly brought up to believe they could do anything they wanted to, even give the executive vice president of a large company feedback on how badly he performed at the assessment center.

Here is another example. My business partner and I were invited to give a talk—for free—to a teenage leadership and community service club that raised money to donate to local causes. We were asked to talk about what leadership qualities are important in the workplace. When we arrived, the club president, who had organized our visit, was not there. She was not on her way either; we were told she was too busy to attend. The club secretary brought us into the room and left us to our own devices. We had to ask to get a projector set up and figure out on our own where we should position it. Meanwhile, a swarm of moms was in the adjoining room, preparing a luxurious spread of food for the teenage club members. After everyone ate, the moms swooped in and cleaned up while the meeting began.

When it was time, the secretary introduced us, but he did not know our names or what we were going to talk about. He said we could introduce ourselves. We got started with an interactive presentation that required club members to participate right away by walking around the room and examining provocative quotes on leadership. We were surprised to find that only about half the students got out of their chairs. We had to personally invite each seated person to participate. And even then, not all of them did. We continued on with the presentation even though many of our audience members were chatting with each other, typing on their laptops, and doing homework. When we were done, we were told we could leave while they continued with club business. We quietly gathered our belongings and snuck out the door.

There was no "thank you." We never heard from the club president by e-mail or any other way to thank us for our pro bono appearance or give us the feedback we asked for. We finally e-mailed her to follow up and did not hear back. We then e-mailed her mom (who we knew) and got a simple report that people liked the presentation.

How does this story relate to perfectionism? Clearly it is not an example of perfectionism in action. In fact, it is quite the opposite. The reason this story is relevant to perfectionism is that it illustrates how much pressure kids are under to have perfect résumés. Surely, being the president of a leadership club looks appealing to college admissions officers. What they don't know, however, is how poorly the work may be getting done. The kids seemed to be in it only for the required "community service" hours. They got a nice dinner, had time to do their homework and chat with their friends, and got to check off two hours of community service. Yes, there was a handful of them who showed some enthusiasm for our talk and the subject matter of the club. The rest, however, looked tired and preoccupied.

I wondered, after this experience, how much these teenagers learned from running this club. Did they learn how to effectively run meetings, make progress, and interact with leaders in the community? Or did they learn it really doesn't take any effort at all to run a club, community service is a joke, and Mommy will take care of us?

Let's apply this to the workplace. I have given a number of talks to professional organizations, including industry groups, community groups, and leadership groups. In every case, I have received either a small gift or a written letter of appreciation. I have always been met by the person who contacted me or been informed well in advance that I would have another contact at the location. People have never chatted through one of my presentations. Admittedly, some professionals have popped out due to "urgent" calls or e-mails, but they are discreet, and they usually apologize. Also, equipment does not always work according to plan, and delays occur. Rarely do things go perfectly, but they usually go professionally. And when they don't, it is very noticeable.

In the workplace (and everywhere, really) people have reputations to uphold. I can't emphasize how important your reputation is in the workplace. People notice what you do (even if it's not posted online). They notice if you get the details right, if you dress appropriately, if you turn in sloppy work, if you don't show up when you say you will. You don't get perfect performance reviews for imperfect work. The stakes are higher at work than at school. If you lead a project and don't get results, there are consequences. You can't complain to the teacher to raise your grade. People notice when the road isn't finished, when the product is not on the shelves, when the judge denies your poorly researched legal brief, and when the drug does not meet FDA approval. At work, it's not just about filling in a résumé; it's about people's and companies' livelihoods. Your work product may not have to be perfect, but it really does need to be good.

In sum, it is important to know when excellence and even perfection are necessary and to follow through in these cases. When the details are not important, it is not worth stressing out over them or expecting excessive praise for doing a job that was good enough but not great. What won't get you anywhere is to think you are perfect and not really do the work. You may get away with that for a little while, but ultimately, you won't fool anyone but yourself (and maybe your parents).

Authenticity

REAL Life

Resilient
Empowered
Authentic
Limber

When we speak of imperfectionism, we are also speaking about authenticity. To be authentic is to be honest with yourself and with others. The first step in being honest with yourself is to make an accurate assessment of your strengths and weaknesses. Yes, you do have weaknesses; we all do. It's better to embrace them and try to develop them than to deny their existence. Only through becoming aware of yourself and your limitations can you be transparent with others.

It seems scary to admit your limitations, but it is actually a huge relief. It is so much easier to know you don't have to be perfect. Suddenly, you can accept yourself for who you are and not criticize yourself for not being able to do it all. You can also tell people what you are good at and where you have limitations to help set their expectations of you. What a relief it is to not have to be perfect for others too! Not only is it a load off your shoulders, but it is a great way to improve communication and collaboration with others. For example, one leader told his team he was incredibly shy inside. He had spent years overcoming his shyness, but it was still there inside him. He said he needed time to get to know his team members. His team was grateful to know how to deal with their leader, and he was relieved to be able to be himself.

Authenticity is covered in more detail in Chapter 6: Polish Communication Skills. The exercises in Part 3 will help you become more self-aware and authentic. They will help you identify your imperfections and embrace them. So will the next chapter, which focuses on resilience.

CHAPTER 4

Build Resilience

Recently, a friend of mine posted the following poem on Facebook. She said her seventh-grade teacher made the class memorize it, and it had helped her get through tough times in her life. Wow, what a great teacher!

Don't Quit

When things go wrong, as they sometimes will,
When the road you're trudging seems all uphill,
When the funds are low and the debts are high,
And you want to smile, but you have to sigh,
When care is pressing you down a bit,
Rest, if you must, but don't you quit.

Life is queer with its twists and turns,
As every one of us sometimes learns,
And many a failure turns about,
When he might have won had he stuck it out;
Don't give up though the pace seems slow—
You may succeed with another blow.

Often the goal is nearer than,
It seems to a faint and faltering man,
Often the struggler has given up,
When he might have captured the victor's cup,
And he learned too late when the night slipped down,
How close he was to the golden crown.

Success is failure turned inside out—
The silver tint of the clouds of doubt,
And you never can tell how close you are,
It may be near when it seems so far,
So stick to the fight when you're hardest hit—
It's when things seem worst that you must not quit.

—Author unknown

I have worked with business leaders for a long time. I have found that the best leaders have had failures and learned from them. They are also open about their failures, rather than covering them up. For example, I saw the CEO of a biotech company give a presentation at a leadership conference, and he started out the talk by telling the audience a little bit about himself. He said he had started out as a lawyer at a law firm, and it was a mutually beneficial decision for him to move out of law and into business. In other words, he was saying he wasn't the best lawyer.

I've known other people who have gotten law degrees and were not well-suited to be lawyers after all. They fled the profession and had a sore spot about it ever after. They made a mistake and were not able to overcome it, learn from it, and move on. Instead, it weakened them.

"Blockbuster turned out to be the worst investment I ever made."
—Carl Icahn, investor, business mogul, worth over $11 billion in 2011 and $20 billion in 2013 (Icahn 2011)

What Does Resilience Look Like in the Workplace?

"My experience is that we learn much more from failure than we do from success."
—A. G. Lafley, former Procter & Gamble CEO

Successful business leaders tell us over and over again that they had to fail to get to where they are. In fact, it is precisely those failures that led to their success. Look at Steve Jobs. When did he come up with the iPod? After he had been kicked out of Apple! When you think of him, do you think of his mistakes? Probably not. You think of his successes: the Macintosh, the iPod, iTunes. Arthur Rock, one of Apple's board members, said, "The best thing ever to happen to Steve is when we fired him, told him to get lost" (Isaacson 2011). The tough love gave him the opportunity to become wiser and more mature. At Next (his subsequent company), Jobs made a series of magnificent products that were complete market flops. These brilliant failures helped him create the great successes he had when he came back to Apple. Steve Jobs is a legendary example of a resilient man.

A recent issue of *Harvard Business Review* was dedicated entirely to the topic of failure, how to understand it, learn from it, and recover from it. The key message from these articles was that successful people not only learn from their mistakes, but they take risks and make mistakes along the way.

Ignatius posits that failure is the best teacher in modern business. "For some entrepreneurs, it's virtually a badge of honor to have stumbled, even spectacularly, on the way to success. Most of us, however, find it hard to draw useful lessons from our missteps. We tend to fail at failure" (Ignatius 2011).

Of course, some mistakes are better to make than others. Unrecoverable mistakes, "stupid" mistakes, foreseeable mistakes, repeated mistakes, deviant or intentional mistakes, and harmful mistakes are worse than "honest" mistakes, unavoidable mistakes, educated guesses, and mistakes under challenging or ambiguous circumstances (Edmondson 2011). Think about it. When do you blame someone for making a mistake? When *don't* you blame them? The tendency is to blame more than we ought to, mostly because we are conditioned to do that. The fear of blame is often a reason for avoiding making mistakes. But if you think about it, there are a lot of mistakes we can make that are not really blameworthy. For example, think about the reasons that a student could fail a test, and look at the figure below.

Mistakes at School Less Blameworthy	More
• Bombed a test that he studied really hard for because the test was really hard **Challenging Task**	• Bombed a test because he was too busy chatting on Facebook to study the night before **Deviance**
• Bombed a test in a class she took to see if she might want to major in that field **Exploration**	• Bombed a test that she studied really hard for because she didn't read the essay question carefully **Inattention**
• Bombed a test because he thought he could write an essay about what he truly believed even though it opposed the teacher's approach **Hypothesis Testing**	• Bombed a test that he studied hard for but he just couldn't understand the material **Lack of Ability**

The same principles hold true at work. The figure below shows some quite impactful mistakes, but again, some are more blameworthy than others. In the business world, we would even call some of these mistakes praiseworthy. In fact, all the ones on the left are praiseworthy.

The doctor tried but was overcome by the challenging task. The marketing manager was trying to expand the company's market share in a new line of business. The researcher was looking for new ways to treat people but hadn't found the right combination yet. They are all situations in which failure is okay—more than okay. The doctor may have learned something new to try next time, or at least learned more about her limitations in saving lives. The marketing manager had the opportunity to learn more about customer desires. The researcher eliminated one combination and may land on the right one next time. Notice that it is important to learn from mistakes no matter what the reason is for making them.

Mistakes at Work **Less**	**Blameworthy** **More**
• The patient died on the operating table because she had so many injuries the surgeon couldn't contain them all quickly enough. **Challenging Task**	• The pilot crashed the plane because he was still drunk from the night before. **Deviance**
• The product failed because the marketing manager was testing customer reactions in a brand-new market. **Exploration**	• The annual report earnings figure was off by a factor of ten because the accountant didn't double-check the numbers before he sent it to the printer. **Inattention**
• The new drug trial failed because it did not heal as many people as it needed to within the researcher's sample. **Hypothesis Testing**	• The narcissistic CEO drove the company to bankruptcy because she was unable to admit she was wrong. **Lack of Ability**

In the workplace, we talk about creating a learning culture. For example, at WD-40, mistakes have been eliminated. Instead, they have what they call "learning moments" (Blanchard and Ridge 2009). An employee could lose the company money and report back to his manager that he had a "learning moment" without ill effect. The manager would be trained to help the employee talk through what he learned. He would share what he learned, as appropriate, to help others in the company grow, as well. This approach encourages employees to take sensible risks that ultimately benefit the company through employee learning and process and product improvement.

Toyota similarly encourages employees to learn from their mistakes. Its company culture is based, in part, on the concept of continuous improvement, called *kaizen* in Japanese (Liker and Hoseus 2008). When there is a problem on the assembly line, for example, an employee pulls a cord that stops the line and rings a bell for a manager. The manager does not come onto the manufacturing floor and yell at the employee. Rather, the manager congratulates the employee and works with him or her to discover the root source of the problem (a process called *genzi genbutso*, or "go to the source"). They continue to work on the problem to fix it, learn from it, and share the new information with others to help them learn too.

Not all companies are run so effectively. Some have dysfunctional cultures in which people are afraid to tell their managers when they make mistakes for fear of being yelled at or even fired. Instead, they either cover them up or fail to take risks at all to avoid making mistakes as much as possible. These types of environments don't tend to foster the success WD-40 and Toyota have enjoyed. They are also miserable places to work.

Renewal

Resilient people take care of themselves. They have to, or they won't be resilient anymore. What does it mean to take care of yourself? It means realizing when you are run down and taking time out to renew. It is not easy for high achievers to recognize they need to take a break and take care of themselves. Leaders in organizations are some of the biggest culprits of running themselves into the ground and taking others down with them. We, as leadership coaches, often have to work with them on self-renewal techniques.

Leaders—and, frankly, people at all positions in the hierarchy of today's fast-paced ever-demanding workplace—are giving of themselves constantly. Company goals of increasing productivity and profits tend to directly oppose employee needs for self-renewal. Actually, it's not the goals themselves but the approaches companies use that oppose employee well-being. In fact, renewal helps increase productivity and profits, but the bulk of stockholders, media, and corporate boards don't seem to understand that. They seem to care only about short-term gains that actually thwart employee and company well-being. Organizations tend to value destructive behavior and mediocre leadership that gets results, any results, no matter the long-term consequences. Unfortunately, schools and colleges are following suit.

How do we renew ourselves to be able to sustain high-level outputs?

"Great leaders are awake, aware, and attuned to themselves, to others, and to the world around them. They commit to their beliefs, stand strong in their values, and live full, passionate lives. Great leaders are emotionally intelligent and they are *mindful*: they seek to live in full consciousness of self, others, nature, and society. Great leaders face the uncertainty of today's world with *hope*: they inspire through clarity of vision, optimism, and a profound belief in their—and their people's—ability to turn dreams into reality. Great leaders face sacrifice, difficulties, and challenges, as well as opportunities, with empathy and *compassion* for the people they lead and those they serve" (Byatzis and McKee 2005).

What Does Resilience Look Like for Youth and Their Parents?

Definition of resilience:

"Resilient youngsters feel special and appreciated. They have learned to set realistic goals and expectations for themselves. They have developed the ability to solve problems and make decisions and thus are more likely to view mistakes, hardships, and obstacles as challenges to confront rather than as stressors to avoid. They rely on productive coping strategies that are growth-fostering rather than self-defeating. They are aware of their weaknesses and vulnerabilities, but they also recognize their strong points and talents. They have developed effective interpersonal skills with peers and adults alike. They are able to seek out assistance and nurturance in a comfortable, appropriate manner from adults who can provide the support they need. Finally, they are able to define the aspects of their lives over which they have control and to focus their energy and attention on these rather than on factors over which they have little, if any, influence" (Brooks and Goldstein 2001).

For Parents

"It is easier to build strong children than to repair broken men."
—Frederick Douglass

Resilient children do not need their parents. That may be an overstatement, but you get the idea. Self-reliant people are empowered to take care of their problems themselves, and they have the inner strength to take risks, make mistakes, and learn from them. As children become more resilient, they need their parents less, and the parents do not feel as needed. That does not feel good to parents who thrive on feeling needed by their children. In other words, developing resilient children is a hard lesson for both parents and kids. The children have to be left on their own to get through difficult experiences, and the parents don't get to rescue them. It is tough on both sides, but children and parents are stronger as a result.

The *New York Times Magazine* published an article saying that one of the ultimate goals of parenting is to make themselves unnecessary, and that may be getting forgotten in today's times. It may not feel good to become unnecessary, and parents may resist it for that reason. At the same time, one of the most important aspects of parenting of children—teens, in particular—is to help them become self-reliant so they can survive on their own as they go off to college and get jobs. The article encourages parents to work on the parenting techniques that encourage self-reliance at this critical time (Belkin 2010).

Preventing children from failing stunts their growth. I was at a toddler's birthday party several years ago, and the moms were trying to come up with some games for the kids to play. One mom suggested musical chairs. "Great idea!" the rest of us said. We gathered up a number of chairs and got some music set up on a portable CD player. The youngsters started to play and the music stopped. I went to remove a chair and a couple moms stopped me. They said the kids were too young to lose. I backed off, and the music started again. The toddlers walked around the chairs and sat down again when the music stopped. The moms cheered them on. The third time, the toddlers got bored and started wandering off. There was no point to the game.

Games have a purpose—to teach children real-life lessons in a safe and fun environment. It is oh-so-tempting as parents to let the children win, but doing that does not help them learn to lose. Of course, I do not recommend playing your most competitive game and pummeling your children every time. That would be silly. But giving them the lesson that "you win some, you lose some" helps them deal with the realities of life. Unstructured playtime is also an important way for children to learn about life, as well as academics.

Another important lesson is to not over-celebrate wins. A karate teacher once told me it was important not to go out and celebrate when our daughter earned her next belt. He said it was important for her to have the satisfaction of earning it for herself and not to earn it for praise and external gratification. Whoops. We were about to take her out for an ice cream. This same karate teacher told me that invariably some kids fail the test to earn their next-level belt. He does not "give the belts away." If a child does not earn the belt, he or she has to wait for the next test and try again. Yes, this is a hard lesson for kids to learn—especially the young ones—but they do learn it, and you can watch them work harder to earn the belt the next time (if the parents do not pull them out of the class).

Martial Arts at the United Studios of Self Defense

The martial arts instructors (called "senseis") at the United Studios of Self Defense (USSD) are some of the best parent coaches I have met. Yes, they are great martial arts instructors too, but they go above and beyond to help parents insist that their children follow the five principles of effort, etiquette, sincerity, self-control, and character outside of the dojo, as well. During class, senseis give children examples of how to practice these principles at home and at school, not just in the martial arts. For example, they will tell the kids to say, "Yes, Mom," when their mother asks them to do something, like clean their room. They tell them to do it the first time Mom asks, not after Mom gets exasperated.

I've also seen moms call the senseis for advice on how to deal with a difficult situation at home, and I've seen the senseis get on the phone and talk to the children to back up Mom. Senseis are great people to have on your side. They command a certain level of respect, and the kids learn very quickly what they *can't* get away with.

Martial arts in general are a great way to develop self-discipline and resilience. There is nothing like learning how to take the

punches to build inner strength, and how important it is to *not* throw the punches when you feel like it to build self-discipline. Even standing still in a straight line in "front position," with your hands clasped together at chest height, builds self-discipline, character, and resilience. It is tough for anyone, let alone a child, to stand completely still for any period of time. It is also hard to hold up your elbows and hands at chest level for a period of time. Your shoulders start to ache. What a lesson in resilience though. Sometimes you have to take a little bit of pain to get through a situation.

Other sports teach this lesson too. The difference at USSD, however, is that the parents are not welcome to butt in and take care of their children. During class, parents must stay outside of the dojo, and children do not have breaks to run over to them for water and snacks. They need to get through class on their own. During tests, parents are not even allowed in at all. The first time I experienced this, I had a passing moment of concern. I was leaving my young daughter with a muscular man who was trained to kill? The sensei laughed at me and said, "Are you kidding? I've got a room full of kids in there. If even one of them says something bad about me, my career is over." Plus, there were several other instructors in there helping out. The idea was for the children to get through the test on their own, without parental support. Often, according to the sensei, kids end up crying during the test, but that is okay. They get through it on their own, and they are proud of their accomplishment. They earned their belt all by themselves.

My husband and I felt useless during this first test. We ended up going out for brunch at a restaurant down the street. The next time, we looked forward to having a couple hours together, just the two of us, no kids.

Character

"The most important thing about leadership is your character and the values that guide your life."
—Brenda Barnes, CEO of Sara Lee

When parents shelter their kids from failure, disappointment, and scary things, they encourage their children to grow up weak and unable to handle such circumstances. At the same time, when parents put a great deal of emphasis on winning, the fear of losing can be overwhelming. If losing—or getting a less-than-perfect grade or not getting accepted to the youth symphony orchestra—is not an option, kids turn to desperate measures. As noted previously, cheating, performance drugs, and even suicide have increased dramatically over the past decades.

Dr. Levine is a psychotherapist who treats teens. She says the following about the privileged teens she has counseled:

"Regardless of how successful these kids look on the surface, regardless of the clothes they wear, the cars they drive, the grades they get, or the teams they star on, they are not navigating adolescence successfully at all. Modest setbacks frequently send them into a tailspin. A talented thirteen-year-old seriously considers hacking his way into the school computer system to raise his math grade. An academically outstanding sixteen-year-old thinks about suicide when her SAT scores come back marginally lower than she had expected. A fourteen-year-old boy cut from his high school junior varsity basketball team is afraid to go home, anticipating his father's disappointment and criticism. He calls his mother, and tells her that he is going to a friend's house. In fact, he is curled up on my couch, red-eyed and hopeless. He believes he has nothing to live for. While it is tempting to attribute scenarios like these to the histrionics of adolescence, it would be a mistake. Adolescent suicide has quadrupled since 1950" (Levine 2006).

Character is an overarching concept that describes many of the traits and skills that are necessary to succeed in the world, including resilience (Josephson, KIPP, GRIT, etc.). The Joseph & Edna Josephson Institute of Ethics is a nonprofit organization in Los Angeles that educates children and adults about ethics and character. It formed the "Character Counts!" Coalition to help organizations educate children and society on how to build character. The institute has defined six pillars of character: (1) trustworthiness, (2) respect, (3) responsibility, (4) fairness, (5) caring, and (6) citizenship. Participating public and private schools across America implement these pillars using the institute's "Character Counts!" program (Josephson, Peter, and Dowd 2001).

How does resilience factor into the six pillars of character? Here are some examples.

- ***Trustworthiness*** *(be honest, reliable, and loyal).* It takes resilience to keep someone's secret when people are pestering you to tell them about it.
- ***Respect*** *(show sincere regard for the worth of people).* It takes resilience to be respectful to someone who is not treating you with respect in return.
- ***Responsibility*** *(do what you are supposed to do, be self-disciplined, and use self-control*). It takes resilience to admit you made a mistake and face the consequences.
- ***Fairness*** *(play by the rules, don't take advantage of others).* It takes resilience to deal with unhappy friends who do not like the outcome of a decision you based on fairness, not favoritism.
- ***Caring*** *(be kind and forgiving, and express gratitude to others).* It takes resilience to care for someone who has hurt you.
- ***Citizenship*** *(do your share to make your organization and community better).* It takes resilience to continue to be a part of a group even when you disagree with its current actions.

Responsibility is the overarching key to character. Being responsible involves all the other pillars and depends on a person's self-control, self-discipline, and resilience.

"We tell lies when we are afraid ... afraid of what we don't know, afraid of what others will think, afraid of what will be found out about us. But every time we tell a lie, the thing that we fear grows stronger."
—Tad Williams, writer, musician, radio host

KIPP's long-standing motto—"Work hard. Be nice."—isn't just a tagline. Since KIPP's beginning in 1994, the development of character has been as important to us as the teaching of rigorous academic skills (KIPP Foundation 2013).

The Knowledge Is Power Program (KIPP) charter schools are a group of 125 public lower, middle, and high schools in the United States. The schools were started by Mike Feinberg and Dave Levin in 1994 to prepare underprivileged children for college. They focus heavily on academic preparation but also have a very strong emphasis on character. In fact, the KIPP schools were the first to have a "character report card" in addition to an academic report card for each student.

Levin tracked alumni from the schools and found the ones who finished college were not necessarily the most academically successful at KIPP. Rather, he found they had exceptionally strong character. "They were the ones who were able to recover from a bad grade and resolve to do better next time; to bounce back from a fight with their parents; to resist the urge to go out to the movies and stay home and study instead; to persuade professors to give them extra help after class" (Tough 2011).

Levin worked with researchers at Penn State and other universities to develop the character report card based on Angela Duckworth and colleagues' (2007) "Grit Scale." Together, they reduced the Grit Scale items to seven factors that significantly predict life satisfaction and high achievement: (1) zest, (2) grit, (3) self-control, (4) social intelligence, (5) gratitude, (6) optimism, and (7) curiosity. They define these character elements as follows:

- Zest: approaching life with excitement and energy, feeling alive and activated
- Grit: finishing what one starts, completing something despite obstacles, a combination of persistence and resilience
- Self-control: regulating what one feels and does, being self-disciplined
- Social intelligence: being aware of motives and feelings of other people and oneself, including the ability to reason within large and small groups
- Gratitude: being aware of and thankful for opportunities that one has and for good things that happen
- Optimism: expecting the best in the future and working to achieve it
- Curiosity: taking an interest in experience and learning new things for its own sake, finding things fascinating (KIPP Foundation 2013)

Grit is a concept developed by Duckworth and colleagues to describe a particular character trait that predicts high achievement. They define grit as "perseverance and passion for long-term goals" or "focused effort and interest over time." They conducted many studies with thousands of participants and concluded that the achievement of difficult goals requires not only talent but also the sustained and focused application of talent over time. Examples of achievement include: military cadets completing training, completion of college and university degrees, grade point average while in college, and fewer career changes over a lifetime. They found that grit is not related to intelligence. However, grittier people with lower intelligence may attain greater achievement, such as a higher GPA, than less gritty people of higher intelligence. In other words, hard work can pay off (Duckworth et al. 2007).

Character building seems to have taken off more easily at the schools for underprivileged children than at schools for privileged kids. It has been more appealing to students who have a real fear of not finishing college, since it offers them a tangible solution they can embrace: work hard, work through challenges, be strong, have strong principles, and you will succeed. Privileged students, on the other hand, do not fear dropping out of college; they take it as a "given" that they will get into college and complete it because everyone in their family does this. The privileged children and parents don't seem to be worried about the increases in emotional problems, burnout, and suicide among affluent children.

Dominic Randolph is the headmaster of Riverdale Country School, one of New York City's most prestigious private schools. He has boldly gone against the trends of today's prestigious schools by eliminating AP tests and limiting homework. More importantly, however, he has been trying to make changes to the character initiatives they have at the school, because he fervently believes that is the missing link to success. Randolph also has worked with the researchers at Penn State and elsewhere, similar to Levin at KIPP, but has taken a more subtle approach to improving character at Riverdale. He stopped short of implementing a character report card because, as he says, "with my school's specific population, at least, as soon as you set up something like a report card, you're going to have a bunch of people doing test prep for it. I don't want to come up with a metric around character that could then be gamed. I would hate it if that's where we ended up" (Duckworth et al. 2007).

Randolph and the teachers at Riverdale face the challenge of overprotective and overzealous parents. For example, K. C. Cohen, a Riverdale guidance counselor, said in the middle school, "If a kid is a C student, and his parents think that he's all-A's, we do get a lot of pushback: 'What are you talking about? This is a great paper!' We have parents calling in and saying, for their kids, 'Can't you just give them two more days on this paper?' Overindulging kids, with the intention of giving them everything and being loving, but at the expense of their character—that's huge in our population. I think that's one of the biggest problems we have at Riverdale" (Tough 2011). The Riverdale administrators suggest the problem with pushing for character at a private school is that you are criticizing the parents (aka your employers). You can see their dilemma. It is not stopping Randolph though. He just has to tread lightly.

Parents, beware!

I was at a character-building workshop with a director of athletics for several school districts in the state of California. He said it was the adults who need character development more than the children. At sports events, he has seen the parents, in particular, demonstrate egregious behavior. One mother actually got arrested because she wouldn't follow the "no backpack" policy at a game. She refused to leave it in her car, argued with the security personnel, and ended up assaulting a police officer, right there in front of her own child and all the other children at the game.

"To ignore evil is to become an accomplice to it."
—Dr. Martin Luther King Jr., civil rights leader

Handling Bullying

Why has bullying become such a serious problem in the United States? Has bullying gotten worse over the years? Some would argue that it has. With the Internet, bullies can have far-reaching effects. Columbine and other extraordinarily violent acts are drawing attention to victims of bullying, showing how much it really can destroy a person. Increases in suicide rates among victims of bullying would also suggest that bullying has gotten worse over the years. However, statistics on bullying prevalence don't match these interpretations.

Susan Engel and Marlene Sandstrom, professors of psychology at Williams College, wrote an op-ed in the *New York Times* on bullying not so long ago (Engel and Sandstrom 2010). Their research indicates that bullying has always existed and children are not meaner than they used to be. They contend what has changed—in the school system, at least—is the shift from teaching skills to live together in a community to teaching skills for passing standardized tests. They advocate community building at schools and emphasizing respect and kindness as a part of the culture of the community, rather than drafting laws to punish bullies. To build a kinder culture, the whole school needs to participate, including teachers, administration, and staff. Role modeling is key to changing a culture.

Insisting on kindness, however, is not enough. Human nature will prevail. There will always be people who are either born with a mean streak or been made domineering by their environment. Natural selection will also continue to exist; not everyone can be a winner. Competition for power, prestige, resources, and affection will continue to exist. In fact, that is precisely what our individualistic capitalist society is built on: competition. There will always be people who will do what they can to get ahead. Even if we all agree to be nice to each other, cheaters will sneak in and will only sometimes get caught. Decades of social psychological research have shown this to be true.

While it certainly is a worthwhile goal to get us to be nicer to each other, we also need to develop resilience and self-defense skills to deal with the situations when people are not nice. Self-defense doesn't necessarily have to be physical; words can be a very strong method, as well. The self-defense program "Play It Safe" teaches that your voice is your strongest tool. Whatever tool you use, it is important to know you have options and the confidence to use them. Sadly, today's parenting trends disempower children, leaving them vulnerable and sometimes incapable of handling even the slightest amount of aggression.

"Tough times never last, but tough people do."
—Robert H. Schuller

Think about it. How many times have you either heard of or been a part of a situation similar to the following? A mother of a nine-year-old picked up her daughter from school. The daughter was crying. One of the girls in the class was having a birthday party and did not invite her. The celebrant and the girls who were invited sat together at the lunch table and talked loudly about the party in front of the girls who were not invited, obviously intending to hurt their feelings. It worked. What did this mom do? She called the mother of the birthday girl and insisted she invite her daughter to the party. Do you think that solved the problem? What are the possible scenarios of how the girls treated her daughter at the birthday party? What lesson(s) might it have taught her daughter?

For Youth

"Success is to be measured not so much by the position that one has reached in life as by the obstacles which have been overcome while trying to succeed."
—Booker T. Washington

This section is written for youth to read. Parents and others can read it too, but it is important for the youth to get these messages. First, did you know that parents and teachers can be overprotecting you by taking care of you, making decisions for you, removing obstacles for you, and solving problems for you? It might be scary for you to try things on your own because you are afraid of failing. But failing is an important component of learning. Read on to find out how you can and should fail.

Risk Taking and Failure

What happens if you make a mistake or, worse, fail?

> **Marshall was on the varsity basketball team senior year in high school. He had been offered a basketball scholarship for the college he wanted to go to. He was feeling pretty good about himself as he caught the ball from his teammate and made the shot. It went in with only twelve seconds left in the game! But his team members looked surprised, not happy. The spectators were yelling like crazy, but he couldn't hear what they were saying. What was wrong? A guy from the other team said, "Thanks, man!" Then it hit him like a fist in the stomach. He had shot the ball into the wrong basket, giving the *other* team two points. They were going to lose the game. His life as he knew it seemed like it was ending too.**
>
> **How big of a mistake was this? What might the consequences be for Marshall?**
>
> **How could you recover from this? Run away and hide, quit the team, joke about it, apologize, bring cookies to next practice, wash the towels ...**

Many students and parents believe if you make even one mistake—get one low grade, lose one game, stay out past curfew—you will lose it all, fall out of the race, and never be able to get back in again. That is just not true! In fact, it is far from the truth. WD-40 Company is a great example of this. As previously noted in the Parents section, at WD-40, they do not make mistakes; instead, they have "learning moments." When employees at WD-40 make a mistake, they openly tell their manager. Employees who have "learning moments" are not punished or humiliated. The point is to learn and improve. At WD-40, a certain amount of risk taking is encouraged to achieve outstanding results, and employees learn from the failures along the way. After all, how do you think WD-40 (the lubricant) was invented in the first place? Check Wikipedia for the interesting story.

> **This invention was a mistake.**
>
> **"The first breakthrough came on 2 June—because of a mistake. The inventors set up a telegraph circuit between two rooms. Alec [Alexander Graham Bell] was in the transmitter room with three sending reeds, while Thomas [Thomas Watson] sat with the receiver. When one of the steel reeds at Thomas' end got stuck, he pinged it free with his finger. Suddenly Alec let out a delighted yell. The matching reed at his end had received the signal and twanged faintly. The sound had been turned into electricity, sent along the wire, and turned back into sound. At that moment the telephone was born" (Hepplewhite 2001).**

What do mistakes get you? Think about it for a moment. Here are some responses to that question: knowledge of what does not work and, more importantly, resilience. You gain knowledge and resilience by taking risks and making mistakes. To start building resilience, try looking at the mistakes you have already made and what you have learned from them. I will start with an example of one of my mistakes.

The biggest mistake I ever made with my career was to major in electrical engineering in college. Even though I was good at math and computers, I was not a very good engineer! In fact, I hated being an engineer! I did it for the wrong reasons. Guess why I went into engineering. Money! Yes, indeed, I did make a lot of money, but I was not happy. In the end, however, being an engineer was a huge contributor to my success. I learned so much from that experience, and it helps me be a better leadership consultant today. As an engineer, I realized how much engineers needed to learn communication skills; that is what helped me decide to become a leadership consultant.

A couple years ago, during a coaching session, an executive told me I had found my calling. It was the best compliment I have ever received at work. I realized then and there that my strength and passion are to help people reach their potential in life. I went through countless failures to get to that point, and it has not been easy.

Reflection:

What is the biggest mistake you have ever made in your life? What did you learn from it?

After learning from the past, it is time to work on the future. How do you build resilience? As Nike says, "Just Do It!" Start taking risks and making decisions on your own. Before you start, however, let's talk through two qualifiers. First, it is important to acknowledge just doing it can be very scary. Fear of failure, fear of success, and fear of the unknown can be very strong for some people, especially if you are not used to it. There's no doubt about it: taking risks requires courage. That brings us to the second point.

"Courage is not the absence of fear. It is going forward with the face of fear."
—Abraham Lincoln

The second qualifier is: be smart about it. Don't take stupid risks, like do drugs or steal a car. Take calculated risks. Start with small risks. Smaller risks have smaller consequences and smaller fears. For example, if you wanted to overcome a fear of heights, you wouldn't start by skydiving. You might start by walking up a staircase (smaller risk, smaller fear). If it's not a phobia you want to overcome so much as a challenge you want to take, you could start by going on a free-fall ride at an amusement park. Again, this is a smaller risk than jumping out of an airplane, but it gives some of the same sensation. It's a calculated risk, because these rides rarely harm anyone and it's only a slight embarrassment if you shriek in front of your friends or decide at the last minute to skip the ride.

Reflection:

List some smart risks you could take right now. Here are some ideas to get the juices flowing:

- **Give a speech (if you're afraid of public speaking).**
- **Ask someone you don't know (but want to) to go out for lunch with you.**
- **Apply for a job that may be slightly out of reach.**
- **Try out a new look.**

Being Grounded

Peter Senge and his colleagues (Senge et al. 2004) suggest that "presence" is a state in which we truly can be aware of how the world interconnects and what solutions may be needed for the future. They describe the state of presence and how to achieve it in their book of the same name. The book is complicated, and it will likely challenge your way of thinking at a profound level; it is for advanced thinkers, a little too heavy to start with but a fantastic book when you are ready.

In short, they define presence as "leading to a state of 'letting come,' of consciously participating in a larger field for change. When this happens, the field shifts, and the forces shaping a situation can move from recreating the past to manifesting or realizing an emerging future." Presence includes being fully conscious and aware in the present moment. It also includes deep listening, which means being open beyond your preconceptions and historical ways of making sense and letting go of old identities and needing to control. In other words, you are truly aware of the moment, of what is going on outside of your control, and you are not trying to shape your interpretation of what is happening to fit into your preconceived world. You are letting it come to you, rather than trying to control what is happening.

Okay, that was deep. But think about it. As a child, your life has probably been largely about being in control—getting good grades, practicing piano, making a home run, impressing others with your skills, telling your computer and phone what to do, and shutting out unwanted distractions. Being present is the opposite of that. It is just being. It is letting go of everything and seeing what is going on around you. Ironically, even though it sounds like a state of relaxation, it can be very hard work to get there. It is hard to change your habits, and it may take a bit of practice to be able to let yourself go into the moment without trying to control it. And, no, you don't need drugs to do this. In fact, drugs will only get in the way of being present.

Reflection:

Recall a time in your life when you felt most intensely alive and could say with confidence, "This is the real me!" Describe who the real you was at the time. Include the context, who was there, and why you felt comfortable being the real you. Then think about what is stopping you from being the real you at other times.

> **"Each day, as you are tested in the world, you yearn to look at yourself in the mirror and respect the person you see and the life you have chosen to lead. Some days will be better than others, but as long as you are true to who you are, you can cope with the most difficult circumstances that life presents" (George and Sims 2007).**

The Sum Total of Resilience

REAL Life

Resilient
Empowered
Authentic
Limber

Being resilient is hard. Resilience contains many components, including strength, optimism, character, and being grounded. Resilient people take risks and bounce back from failure. They maintain a positive attitude even when times are tough. They don't let themselves get taken down by bullies. They do the right thing even when there is a lot of pressure not to. They take time to ground and renew themselves to top up their energy. The exercises in Part 3 will help you develop resilience. But don't expect to be resilient overnight. You need to build resilience, and that takes time and effort and lots of failures. Make sure to replenish your energy as you work on your resilience.

CHAPTER 5

Develop Independence

The Fear Factor

"I want to do it myself," says the two-year-old as he struggles to pull his shirt over his head. Kids start to assert their independence from a very young age. Sometimes it's endearing, sometimes it's annoying, and other times it's downright dangerous. Endearing is lovely. Annoying is manageable. Dangerous is a judgment call. Is it slightly risky? Is the potential harm tolerable, such as a skinned knee? Could it be stitches or a broken bone? Or would it be certain death? The thoughts that go through parents' heads as their kids run around and "get into things" can be tough. It becomes a problem, however, when parents are overcome with fear that anything a child does on his or her own is dangerous. Unfortunately, our society is rapidly approaching this point.

Profit-driven media, overzealous social workers, ambulance-chasing lawyers, and preying corporate marketing departments have thrust our society against a wall of fear. People are terrified of being held liable for harm to another, especially to a child. It's why we see signs up cautioning us that the ground may be wet when it's raining out. It's why the camp counselors wouldn't let my twelve-year-old daughter open the car door by herself when I dropped her off at camp this summer. It's made parents irrationally fear that something might happen to their kids and that their kids can't be left in an unsecured environment at any time. As a result, kids increasingly participate in supervised, structured, safe activities. They rarely have time to themselves to explore, play, create, and just space out, and they rarely have the opportunity to figure things out for themselves.

Learned Helplessness

"Your passion is waiting for your courage to catch up."
—Marilyn Greist

Even when it doesn't come to safety, have you noticed that parents are doing more and more for their children these days? One mother of a ten-year-old still picks out her daughter's clothes for her every day. She doesn't have confidence in her daughter to choose her own clothes. A seven-year-old boy tells his daddy to put his socks and shoes on for him—and Daddy *does*! Daddy doesn't push back to tell his son that he could do it himself. Whether it's the parents or the children who drive the dependence, it generates adults who don't know how to take care of themselves or their work. This is what managers are complaining about. Young workers need "hand holding" to get them from one step to the next in task completion. How do we raise children to learn how to do it on their own?

Two things have to happen for children to develop into independent people: (1) parents have to let go (of their kids), and (2) kids have to let go (of their parents). It's that simple. But it's not that easy! Parents feel special when they are needed. They also feel special when their "best friends" love them unconditionally. Children feel good when they are taken care of, and it is so much easier if someone else does it for them. In addition, it is scary to let go. It's scary for parents to let their kids try things on their own because they might fail or get hurt in the process. It is scary for kids to try things on their own for the same reasons. It's the discomfort that keeps the codependence in place.

Dealing with Discomfort

Experiencing the discomfort of letting go and trying things out on your own is not fun. Surely you can think of numerous times you have avoided doing something because you didn't want to feel the discomfort. For example, it may be awkward for you to tell an employee that they haven't done a good enough job. It may be heart-wrenching to discipline your child. It may be scary to take the car for a spin on your own for the first time or ask someone out on a date or travel far away to college. We sometimes find ways around doing what we ought to do to avoid the discomfort. We ignore bad behavior, invite others along to accompany us, or decide we didn't really want to do it anyway. We conclude the person's performance wasn't really that bad or choose to go to college closer to home. By doing this, we limit ourselves (and others) to being dependent and accomplishing less.

It takes courage to break through the discomfort. Bill Treasurer describes three primary types of courage in his book, *Courageous Leadership*. Two of them are particularly important in this context: "try courage" and "trust courage" (Treasurer 2011). We need courage to try new things, and we need courage to trust others to do the right thing. It may be scary, but we need to be brave to be independent.

"Courage is acting on what is right, despite being afraid or uncomfortable, when facing situations involving pain, risk, uncertainty, opportunity, or intimidation."
—Bill Treasurer

For Parents

"Children are apt to live up to what you believe of them."
—Lady Bird Johnson

Building Trust with Your Children (or Anyone)

How to develop trust in a relationship:

1. **Prove trustworthiness by doing something extraordinary, or have the other person do it.**
2. **Demonstrate honest behavior over time, and watch to see if the other person does too.**
3. **Structure incentives to encourage cooperation.**
4. **Have a third party act as a go-between, certifying each person's trustworthiness.**
5. **Acquire a shared interest, or a superordinate goal—one that depends on both people's participation to succeed.**
6. **Use a combination of punishment and incentives.**
7. **Break up agreements into smaller components that are less risky (Larson 2004).**

When trust is not a given, engage in "tempered trust":

1. **Start small.**
2. **Include an escape clause.**
3. **Be explicit when you trust and reprimand.**
4. **Recognize the other person's dilemma.**
5. **Look at roles, as well as people.**

Continue to examine whether it is appropriate to trust this person in this role at this time (Kramer 2009).

Your role in building your children's independence is learning to trust them to take care of themselves, gradually, over time. How do you do that? Let's examine trust for a moment. The ability to trust others develops during childhood. It begins with learning to trust ourselves (Reina and Reina 2006). Our ability to trust ourselves affects our attitude toward taking risks and trying new things. Essentially, trusting ourselves is believing in ourselves. If we don't believe in ourselves, we won't try new things. For example, if I don't believe that I am able to write a book, I'll never try to write one. Also, if we don't believe in ourselves, we won't believe in others.

Reflection:

- **How did your trust develop? Did you grow up in a supportive, caring household or one in which you experienced inconsistent care, unsafe situations, or loss?**
- **As an adult, what experiences of trust have you had? Have you experienced honest, caring, reliable partners? Have you been betrayed often or in a big way by people you care about? How about at work?**

As a result of your experiences, how well are you able to trust yourself? How much confidence do you have in yourself? How willing are you to trust others?

It is critical for parents to be able to trust their children. Without trust, parents can't take their eyes off their kids. They either become micromanaging, nagging obstacles that their kids want to avoid at all costs, or they become slaves to spoiled, incapable children who need them to do every little thing for them. While no parent aims to end up in either of these situations, we probably have all been there at one point or another. We may even have paused to scratch our heads and wonder how we got there and how to get out of it.

Whether trusting people comes easily or not, there are some standard ways of building trust, especially for when you're starting with little or no trust. It may be that you aren't inclined to trust or that your child has blown it in the past, or you're embarking on a new phase of their development and you just don't know if they can handle it. Regardless, try the suggestions in the box below.

"Mommy, up!"

In addition to developing our own ability to trust, as parents, we need to help our children develop their ability to trust. Kids need to be able to trust both themselves and others to become independent. As described in the previous chapter, having confidence in yourself is important to being resilient. It's also important to stepping out and trying new things. For kids to develop independence, they need to have a healthy sense of trust. You can enable that or disable that from developing, depending on how you demonstrate trust to your children.

> **"A higher capacity to trust enables us to take risks, particularly during times of change and transition. We are able to deal with uncertainty and ambiguity, try new approaches, take calculated chances, and share pertinent information, to include our thoughts and feelings when appropriate" (Reina and Reina 2006).**

You may think of building trust and confidence as building self-esteem. While this is true, it is not built through blind praise, as many people are doing these days. Confidence and trust in oneself has to come from an honest assessment of what one can accomplish, not an inflated ego. To build a child's confidence, you need to give them honest feedback and encouragement. If you tell them that they are wonderful all of the time—even when they aren't—they will stop trusting in you, not to mention, stop believing in themselves.

For Youth

How do you develop the courage to try new things? I know a child who is afraid to try new foods. She's more afraid than the average person. She will avoid it if at all possible, even if it means missing out on a treat or a meal. When the consequences get so grave or the incentives so great, she might venture out to taste something new. She starts by portioning off the smallest morsel she can possibly get onto a fork without it falling through the cracks. Then she sniffs it. She slowly counts to ten, makes sure no one is looking, and trepidatiously puts it in her mouth. She then chews for what seems like an immeasurable number of times before swallowing. It is certainly a sight to see. The fear and discomfort she experiences from trying a new food are impressive. It's easy to see why she avoids it. Yet if she doesn't try new foods she'll have to live in a very small and lonely world.

For some people, trying new things is invigorating. That's probably why the Bertie Bott's Every Flavour Beans jelly beans from the *Harry Potter* series have been successful. There's always someone who is willing to try the earwax flavor. There is a point, however, where we all experience a certain level of discomfort. There is no easy way around it. Get used to it.

The first step to building independence is to get out of your comfort zone. If you are used to being taken care of by your parents, that will mean to start taking risks and making decisions on your own. When you feel yourself staying inside your comfort zone, ask yourself what you can do to get out of it.

Reflection:

What will you be doing over the next few days, weeks, months? What can you do to take you outside of your comfort zone?

For example, say you are going to Disneyland. What can you do in Disneyland to take you out of your comfort zone? Here are some ideas that may come to mind: ride a scary ride, tell your parents you will see them when you get home (and not text them throughout the day), or buy a silly hat and wear it around for the day.

After you take yourself outside of your comfort zone, take time to reflect on how it went. How scary or uncomfortable was it? How did you feel when it was over? Would you do it again? How did the experience build your resilience for future events that may take you outside of your comfort zone?

On the other hand, developing your independence may be more uncomfortable for your parents than for you. If that's the case, you may have to gently tell your parents that you need to do it on your own. That can be another uncomfortable situation. It may be very difficult for your parents to let go. They might have a lack of trust in you, a lack of trust in the world around you, or simply a need within themselves to keep you by their side. Instead of becoming an impossibly hostile adolescent, I recommend you read the section for parents and help them develop trust in you to be able to take care of yourself. This may be a slow process, but it can be done.

Independent Decision Making

Making decisions is another aspect of independence. To be independent, you need to be able to choose which path to take on your own, without looking for someone else to take the responsibility off your shoulders.

A couple weeks ago, I was coaching a seventeen-year-old girl. During the session, she told me her mother was her best friend. After we finished the session, I saw her with her mother at a reception. She was bombarding her mother with questions such as these:

"Mom, I'm feeling tired. Should I rest or socialize?"

"Should I have something to eat? I'm a little hungry, but I don't know."

"Is this dress okay, or should I change?"

"Mom, should I take up long boarding?"

"Do you think I should like this guy in my math class?"

I thought to myself, *I'd never hire her!*

Don't fall into the temptation of being best friends with Mom or Dad. Mom or Dad cannot be your best friend because they are Mom or Dad. They cannot share that role. When Mom or Dad tells you to do something, they have authority over you. They probably have at least twenty more years of experience than you. It is easy to hand over responsibility to them, but if you keep doing that, you will not be able to live without them.

Reflection:

What decisions do you let your parents make for you? What decisions do you ask for help on? What decisions do your parents make for you without asking you?

If you are not used to making decisions on your own, you may want to start out small by thinking through some of the following questions. What decisions would you feel comfortable making on your own? What are some decisions that you can start making on your own that are low risk? For example, you may not want to start out by deciding which college to go to on your own, but what to pack for your spring break trip. If you forget your toothbrush, you may have bad breath, but it's not as disastrous as choosing a four-year college that isn't right for you. Continue developing your resilience, and build up to that one.

What can you do to get out of the trap of being dependent? When you feel the urge to ask for help, stop and figure it out on your own. Don't end up as one of those college students who calls their mom in the morning to ask them what to wear, or calls their dad to look up directions to the nearest convenience store. On the other hand, the help may be originating from your parents: "Here are the courses you should sign up for this semester," or "I bought this outfit for you to wear at your job interview." If that's the case, you may need to gently tell your parents they need to stop making decisions for you so you can get used to making them on your own.

Also, don't make a mountain out of a molehill. Many people, especially young people, think that their decisions are life-altering. While a very few may be, most of the decisions you make aren't as important as you think. Most decisions can be changed, as well. You can decide one day to be an engineer and the next to be a psychologist. I did! It's not always easy to change your mind, and sometimes you still have obligations to fill before you can move in a different direction, but most of the time it can be done. And, let's face it, most of the decisions you make don't really matter anyway. What should you have for dinner? Should you take Latin or Chinese? Should you take the job in Tucson or Chicago? No matter which path you take, if you are on your road to success, you will get there.

From Independence to Empowerment

REAL Life

Resilient
Empowered
Authentic
Limber

To be empowered is to be liberated. Liberating means letting go. Letting go involves trusting yourself and others to be independent. To succeed in REAL life, you need to have the power within yourself to move forward. Yes, you can depend on others along the way, but if you depend on others entirely, you won't be living your dream; you'll be living theirs. Parents have to let go of their children, and children have to let go of their parents for children to be ready to succeed in REAL life. The exercises in Part 3 will help you develop trust and independence to empower yourself to live the life you want to lead.

CHAPTER 6

Polish Communication Skills

**"It is the province of knowledge to speak,
and it is the privilege of wisdom to listen."
—Oliver Wendell Holmes**

Teamwork has been the norm now for quite a while, and being a team player is an obvious expectation for new employees. What's new, however, is the trend to collaborate across boundaries. What does that mean? It means to work with others outside of your organization. For example, developers at Lego are now working with customers to design new toys. Microsoft works with industry, law enforcement agencies, governments, and NGOs to increase security, privacy, and safety online. Employees in private industry can collaborate with government agencies, NGOs, and people in other industries and other countries with different values, laws, languages, and customs. In this integrated environment, communicating effectively is critically important.

At the same time, technological advances have brought about frenzied lifestyles with information overload: the need for constant connection to the Internet; cell yell in restaurants; urgent e-mails at all hours of the day and night; and texting during meals, in the restroom, and even while driving. We've become dependent on our connectedness. If I leave the house and realize my cell phone is sitting on my desk, I feel a wave of serious panic wash over my body. *Do I have time to turn around and get it? What happens if someone calls? I won't be able to check my e-mail—for a couple of hours, maybe all day, eek!* We have developed a deep insecurity of not being able to be in touch with people whenever we want.

Ironically, this hyper-connectedness is damaging our communication skills. We are so distracted because we are multitasking that we rarely give focused attention to the person at the other end of the communication. We take shortcuts to communicate with each other, like memes and abbreviations in text messages and chats. Our writing skills are plummeting, and our conversation skills are suffering too. Look around you while you're waiting for a show to start or are in line for something. How many people are talking versus texting?

Some people think old-fashioned communication skills are not needed in the modern world. But don't forget that people are people. We still need to interact, understand, and connect with each other. The most important aspect of communicating is not talking but listening. Listening is not just about knowing that sounds are coming out of someone's mouth. It is about hearing the words, seeing the nonverbal cues, and understanding the message.

The Importance of Face-to-Face Interaction

From a case study of telecommuting that I conducted with several colleagues:

A large industrial company with employees in both the United States and Japan has distributed work sites in different regions of the United States that engage in different aspects of design. One of the facilities is a world-renowned design studio that has won several prestigious awards around the globe for its creative designs. The design studio uses a collaborative approach to creative design. In particular, the studio strives to pair up designers with totally different perspectives to create friction, which ultimately produces more creative results. This is important because the employees are involved in conflict, and that influences their interaction styles and communication

practices. Face-to-face interaction is desirable for this type of creative work. Telecommuting is not permitted. If designers are located in different offices, they must travel to work face-to-face.

The engineers suggest that there are many benefits of meeting face-to-face. These include: personal growth (travel and learning), ease of interacting remotely after meeting face-to-face, obtaining a "sense" of the other person, seeing what others are trying to accomplish, facilitating teamwork, establishing personal relationships and friendships, building trust, seeing others' reactions, seeing eye contact and body language, and clearly focusing on the problem without distractions. The industrial designers also report that they need face-to-face interaction to resolve the issues, a lot of communication is nonverbal (like reactions to designs), they want a deeper level of understanding than they get via e-mail, and they have quick access to high-level executives for approvals (often they are at the face-to-face meetings).

Listening

As described in the "For Youth" section in the previous chapter, "presence" is the word we use with executives to convey an advanced form of listening. To listen is to take in and understand what is being communicated to you. To do that effectively, you have to be present. I don't mean physically present in the same room (although that helps). I mean being here and now, focusing on what the person is communicating to you, processing the information you are taking in, and checking in to make sure you have understood. I don't mean "listening" while you check in on Facebook, write your English paper, watch YouTube, and listen to music using earbuds.

Although the "hipster" way of being is to multitask, there are limits to how much parallel processing you can do. Take your computer as an example. Computers are designed to multitask, but if a computer is doing a computation-intensive task, the processing slows down, and sometimes applications stop responding. It is the same with people. I love multitasking. I thrive on it, but I also know when and what I can multitask. For example, I can run the washing machine and the dishwasher at the same time, cleaning both the clothes and dishes simultaneously, while I write. However, I cannot write and talk on the phone at the same time. I will either lose track of the conversation or lose my train of thought about what I am writing. I need to focus.

Think about this from the perspective of when you are trying to communicate with people. How does it make you feel when they drop everything and focus entirely on you? Compare this to when they are paying attention to several other things while you are trying to communicate to them. It feels much different, doesn't it? In addition to improving your ability to understand someone's message, giving someone your full attention is showing them respect and caring. These are the messages you are conveying to them during the interaction.

Active Listening

Active listening is making sure the message you are taking in is the message people are trying to give you. It involves telling people what you think they mean and checking to see if it is what they meant. There is a very simple model to follow to help you be an active listener.

When you are the one sending the message and you think people are not listening, ask them to tell you what their understanding is of what you said. You can say, for example, "I'm not sure I'm getting my point across. Could you tell me what you think I'm trying to say?"

LAR Model **Listen-Acknowledge-Reflect**	**Examples**
Listen	Eye contact, forward posture, no distractions, no interruptions
Acknowledge	Nod, "yes," "uh-huh," "tell me more," "okay"
Reflect	"What I heard you say was [tell it back in your own words]. Is that right?" Example: "What I heard you say is that your car caught on fire on the way to work. Is that right?" "No. What I said was that I got into a car accident on the way to work and then I got fired for being late." "Oh, you got into an accident on the way to work! Are you okay?"

Understanding the Context

Understanding what is being said is only a fraction of the task of communicating. Taking in signals from the entire context is critical. We have all seen movies in which the world is about to end and two people share an intimate moment—then the world doesn't end and they are stuck with what they said to each other. Context is extremely important. When you are communicating with someone, it is important to understand where they are coming from. Are they angry because someone close to them just passed away? Did they just fly in from a foreign country in which the culture is very different from yours? Are their parents listening in on the conversation? Is this a college interview or a casual conversation between friends? People act in very different ways in different situations and depending on what else is weighing on their minds.

Being Focused

To keep yourself from being distracted by the things that may be weighing on your mind and help you focus on what is going on right here and now, it is helpful to ground or center yourself prior to the interaction.

Quotes from Stan Herman on Grounding

"To be grounded is to find the calm place at the center of yourself, while viewing alertly the people and events around you."

"To be grounded is to quiet your mind's frantic search for other appropriate answers."

"To be grounded is to let go of your disconcerting speculations about what the other person is thinking, so that you can focus full attention on what she is communicating. Full attention includes both your clear mind and your serene body."

"Grounded you are secure, have access to your personal power, have the help of your 'greater self' available."
—Stan Herman, author, leadership consultant

Grounding, centering, and meditating all focus on one important thing: eliminating distractions. Grounding is shifting your attention to your sensory inputs to see, hear, smell, taste, and feel what is going on around you. Centering is focusing on your center, whether that is the center of your energy or the center of where you want to be right now. For example, you can center yourself on how you want to show up to a meeting. Meditating can be either emptying your mind of all thoughts or being mindful of each thought and dismissing it from your mind for the present moment. Whether you ground, center, or meditate for hours or minutes, it will help you be more present in interactions with others.

If all this mindfulness and centering stuff sounds too squishy and soft to you, let me put it in terms you might find more appealing. Think about what athletes do before a game, match, or competition. They focus on winning. Many athletes use mental imagery to see themselves winning. Others rely on "flow," which is a state where you are not thinking about what you are doing at all. You let your mind and body work together without cognitive management. Of course, flow is all about focusing on yourself and is not necessarily a mental state you

A Five-Minute Grounding Exercise

There are many resources available to you to help you ground yourself. Books, yoga classes, meditation classes, and videos exist. If you are not inclined to invest a lot of time into this, start out small. Five minutes before a meeting or social interaction can make a big difference. If you can get yourself into a quiet place where you are alone, I recommend closing your eyes and breathing deeply to calm yourself down. If you can't do this, you still can follow this exercise more subtly without closing your eyes or drawing attention to your breathing.

Close your eyes and take a deep breath (counting to three), hold your breath (counting to three), and release the breath (counting to three). As you hold your breath, focus on something in your mind, imagine it as a helium balloon, and let go of it as you slowly release your breath and watch the balloon float away. Let your distracting thoughts float away for the time being. You can always get them back later. Repeat this exercise until your mind is clear of distractions. Make sure to breathe slowly to avoid hyperventilating.

Once you have cleared your mind of distractions, you can focus on what you want to focus on. In a grounding situation, you will want to focus on your sensory inputs, to see, feel, and hear what is going on around you to better connect with others. In a centering situation, you will want to focus on centering your focus on how you want to be in the moment.

want to be in when communicating with others. Performing is when flow would be a useful mental state. In any case, high-level athletes tend to agree that mental focus is the key to winning. It sets the winners apart from the runners-up. Athletes also tend to agree that this type of focus helps them with other aspects of life, as well.

Centering Example

It was Monday morning, and I was on my way to work. We had gone away for the weekend, and I stayed up excessively late Sunday night getting my overstimulated kid to sleep, filling out paperwork for her summer camp, and preparing my presentation for the next day. In the morning, I pried myself out of bed against all natural instincts to sleep, did the same for my daughter as she kicked and screamed, got into a fight with the camp counselor about the incomplete paperwork, and left my daughter in the arms of the pissed-off counselor, shrieking at the top of her lungs how much she needed me. I was fighting against anger, frustration, and exhaustion as I sped into work to give a presentation to a room full of executives on how to manage emotions.

I needed to calm myself down, get myself into presentation mode, and bring my knowledge of emotional intelligence to the forefront of my mind. And I had only a fifteen-minute car ride to do it. How is that possible? With training and practice and a great level of determination, I was able to get myself to a point where I could succeed. Was it the best presentation I ever gave? No, not by far, but I was focused and in the moment.

Obviously, I could not close my eyes and envision balloons of distractions while driving, but I could calm myself down with deep breathing. At stoplights I could briefly close my eyes and focus. While I drove, I could think about how I wanted to come across to the executives. I could run through the basic tenets of emotional intelligence to get the juices flowing. I did just that, and I kept up the deep breathing and centering while I walked from the parking lot to the building. I put the screaming kid aside for the moment, knowing she would be there when I was done. I was ready for the executives.

Is this the ideal centering example? No, but it does show how even just a little bit can go a long way. You can do this too. And imagine the results when you are fully centered!

Trust

- **How can we believe someone with a history of lies?**
- **How can we have faith in someone whose "walk" doesn't match his or her "talk"?**
- **How can we count on someone who doesn't keep promises?**
- **How can we entrust our well-being or interests to someone who has been disloyal?**

Trust greatly facilitates communication. But trust is complicated. You can trust or distrust someone, or hold judgment when you don't have enough information. Extending trust involves risk and vulnerability. Putting your trust in someone leaves you open to disappointment or possibly even harm, depending on the circumstances. Trusting involves using both your head and heart. You can trust people based on your relationship with them or your assessment of their credibility. Let's not forget that trust is a two-way street. To have a trusting relationship, both parties need to trust each other. Therefore, you need to be perceived as trustworthy to engender trust from others.

Why is trust important to organizations? In general, trust is more productive than distrust. The gains from trust can far outweigh the savings from distrust. Research on organizations shows that trust predicts many desirable outcomes, including increased job performance, good citizenship behavior, and commitment to the organization from employees. In turn, that results in increased performance, profitability, and customer satisfaction for the organization. In other words, trust is very important to organizations, and they want to hire employees who are trustworthy and who can trust others. If you want to learn more about trusting others, see the "For Parents" section in the previous chapter on independence. To learn about how to increase other people's trust in you, read on.

Warren Buffett (CEO of Berkshire Hathaway) wanted to acquire McLane Distribution (a $23 billion company) from Wal-Mart. How long does it typically take to merge two public companies like this? And how much does it typically cost? Several months and several million dollars to do the due diligence, verify information, and so on. But, here, because both parties operated with a high level of trust, the deal was made with one two-hour meeting and a handshake. In less than a month, it was completed. Warren Buffet wrote in the 2004 annual report that they did no due diligence. They knew everything would be exactly as Wal-Mart said it would be—and it was (Covey 2006).

To be perceived as trustworthy, it is important to exhibit the behaviors in the table below.

Trustworthy Behaviors	Examples
Behave consistently (be fair and dependable)	Betty asked her English teacher for an extension on a homework assignment because her mother was ill and she had to take care of the family that week. The English teacher agreed because Betty had a history of turning in assignments on time.
Behave with integrity (tell the truth, admit mistakes)	When Agent Madison said she didn't know one of the suspects had fled town, her boss believed her because she had always spoken honestly in the past and admitted when she was wrong.
Share control (give others power too)	Will knew he could bully his way into having total responsibility for the project, but he decided to share ownership with Matt because he knew Matt wanted it too.

Trustworthy Behaviors	Examples
Communicate accurately and thoroughly (share information)	Tom told the vice president of engineering there was a bug in the design he had made and he would come up with a solution by the end of the week.
Demonstrate concern for others (even when it's tough)	Brent saw that Chu was working late every night to finish the project, and he didn't have to. He offered to take on some of Chu's work to even the load.

Trust and communication are inextricably related. Trust helps improve communication, and communication helps build trust. There is a large body of research that shows trust is better built face-to-face than online. This highlights the importance of spending time face-to-face, especially for the younger generation of people who are so hooked on virtual communications. People don't feel as accountable when interacting virtually as they do face-to-face. Also, people aren't able to read others as well online because the nonverbal cues are missing. Once trust has been built, trust may ensue in virtual interactions, but it is harder to build trust that way.

Ten Behaviors to Increase People's Trust in You

1. **Tell the truth.**
2. **Respect others.**
3. **Communicate expectations.**
4. **Share information.**
5. **Deliver results.**
6. **Hold yourself accountable.**
7. **Listen to others.**
8. **Trust others.**
9. **Be loyal to others.**
10. **Make things right when you are wrong (Covey 2006).**

Managing Emotions

Emotions are a critical component of communication. In fact, many researchers believe emotions developed through evolution as a means to communicate with others. Babies learn from infancy how to cry and smile to communicate emotionally with caregivers. As people mature, they learn how to perceive and manage emotions to engage in more sophisticated communications. The extent to which they develop these skills is called "emotional intelligence."

> **Emotional intelligence is the ability to:**
>
> - **perceive emotions;**
> - **assess and generate emotions so as to assist thought;**
> - **understand emotions and emotional knowledge; and**
> - **regulate emotions so as to promote emotional and intellectual growth (Mayer and Salovey 1997).**

To be emotionally intelligent, you have to have skills in four different areas: perceiving emotions, using emotions, understanding emotions, and managing emotions.

- Perceiving emotions means to both physically and cognitively recognize you (or someone else) are experiencing an emotion. For example, you can perceive in yourself that your heart rate has increased, your stomach is fluttering, and you are flushed. That might be nervousness, anger, love, or embarrassment. To perceive an emotion in others, you might see the smile on their face, the crinkle in their brow, and their closed posture and realize they are feigning contentment but are really uncomfortable.
- Using emotions means simply to be able to feel emotions and generate emotions when you want to. For some people, this can be quite difficult. They may have been taught to never be

emotional, so they remain flat and in control in all situations. You can't tell if they are happy or sad.

- Understanding emotions refers to knowing what causes emotions and being able to communicate about emotions articulately. Some people might be able to see you are sad but not understand that insulting your clothing choice caused the sadness to occur.
- Managing emotions is pretty straightforward; it is about managing your own and other people's emotions—the highest level of emotional intelligence. Salespeople, for example, tend to be very good at managing emotions. They can show concern for you and your well-being, as well as pep you up to buy a product. All four components of emotional intelligence are important to building rapport with others and communicating effectively with people.

Emotional intelligence is important to many functions in organizations that are critical to individual and organizational success. For example, emotions are important in managing groups, negotiating solutions, making personal connections, welcoming diversity, inquiring tactfully, listening attentively, collaborating across boundaries, and bringing about change.

Emotional intelligence, contrary to cognitive ability, is learnable. One way to learn how emotionally intelligent you are is to ask people you know. In other words, get some feedback. Don't just ask people who adore you and think you are amazing. Ask people whom you trust to give you honest feedback, perhaps people you do not get along with so well. You'd be surprised what you might learn about yourself.

In addition to soliciting feedback from people you know, you can do an assessment of emotional intelligence using one of many commercial instruments available. (See the exercises for this chapter in Part 3 for some suggestions.) Schools and companies often have access to these tools. Ask someone in human resources or career services to see if you have access to a free instrument. It is better to start early, because lacking the skills to manage emotions can take you off a career track instantly. If you get into a fight with the wrong person, you can be out on your fanny before you know what happened.

Reflection:

- **Are you surprised when other people tell you how they feel? Do you know when they are kidding? Are you generally aware of what emotions you are feeling? These questions all relate to perceiving emotions. Attending to emotions and trying to figure out how people are likely to feel in the situation may help you improve your accuracy in perceiving emotions.**
- **Do you change your mood easily? Can you motivate yourself? Can you excite others? Can you feel what others are feeling—actually *feel* it? These questions all relate to using emotions. Emotions affect the way we think. They can enhance thinking or get in its way. You can use emotions to increase the information you consider in brainstorming or decision making by seeing other perspectives.**
- **Do you find yourself being confused at how "irrational" people's decisions are? Do you talk about emotions? Are you a good judge of others? These questions relate to understanding emotions. By understanding what leads to various emotions, you can improve your predictions of how people will feel and act.**
- **Do you use your feelings (or your gut) to guide you? Do your decisions end well? Are you good at influencing others? These questions relate to managing emotions. Using your emotions judiciously and deliberately—not impulsively—will help you resolve conflict and lead others.**

Authenticity

REAL Life

Resilient
Empowered
Authentic
Limber

One evening several years ago, my husband, daughter, and I were sitting around the kitchen table after dinner. My husband got up, went into the pantry, and shut the door behind him. I heard a bunch of rustling noises, like plastic bags being handled. I couldn't for the life of me figure out what he could possibly be doing in there. Then all of a sudden I remembered I had hidden all the Halloween candy in there. He was eating it! What do you think I did? I "covered" for him in front of my daughter, and then I took a turn! That is exactly what I am *not* talking about when I say we should act authentically. And as I did it, I realized I needed to change my behavior to stay true to my values.

Authenticity is being true to yourself, being open with others, and behaving ethically. In the workplace, we often talk of engaging in transparent communications. The transparency is showing on the outside what is on the inside, not hiding behind a wall of secrecy.

> **"People trust you when you are genuine and authentic, not an imitation."**
> **—Bill George, author of *True North: Discover your Authentic Leadership***

The first step in being authentic is self-awareness. This is also touched on in Chapter 3: Accept Imperfection. You have to know who you are—for better and for worse—and what is important to you to be true to yourself. This may sound easy, but it really isn't. Let me put on my psychologist hat for a moment and talk to you about self-deception. We've all heard about denial, rationalization, repression, and narcissism. And, yes, we all do it. The question is, to what extent? To be authentic, you have to know what your fears and anxieties are and what coping mechanisms you adopted to deal with early childhood experiences that are still in effect today. You have to break through your self-deception and come to terms with yourself. You have to accept your strengths and weaknesses and be willing to share them to interact with and lead people. This is harder for some people than for others. But as I said in Chapter 3, it is such a relief when you do.

I work with a lot of leaders, and I can tell very quickly who is self-aware and who isn't. I am sure you can too, if you think about it. The self-aware leaders are much stronger people, and they are easier to follow because they are consistent and open about their agendas. Steve Jobs was a great role model for authentic leadership when he told three self-revealing stories in his 2005 Stanford commencement address.

An Excerpt from Steve Jobs's 2005 Stanford Commencement Address

"I was lucky—I found what I loved to do early in life. Woz and I started Apple in my parents' garage when I was 20. We worked hard, and in 10 years Apple had grown from just the two of us in a garage into a $2 billion company with over 4,000 employees. We had just released our finest creation—the Macintosh—a year earlier, and I had just turned 30. And then I got fired. How can you get fired from a company you started? Well, as Apple grew we hired someone who I thought was very talented to run the company with me, and for the first year or so things went well. But then our visions of the future began to diverge and eventually we had a falling out. When we did, our Board of Directors sided with him. So at 30 I was out. And very publicly out. What had been the focus of my entire adult life was gone, and it was devastating ...

> **"I didn't see it then, but it turned out that getting fired from Apple was the best thing that could have ever happened to me. The heaviness of being successful was replaced by the lightness of being a beginner again, less sure about everything. It freed me to enter one of the most creative periods of my life" (Jobs 2005).**

Part of being self-aware is to understand what is important to you. I am talking about values. Values include how you think people should be treated, how important honesty is to you, what fairness is, how important money is, how important relationships are, and so on. For example, I had to come to terms with my values when I had a child. When I realized how important it was for me to spend time with my child, I had to reanalyze my career goals. Once you know what your values are, you can rank them in order of importance. Then you can translate them into principles by which you behave. (See the exercises for this chapter in Part 3 for an exercise on this topic.)

Once you know who you are and what you value, the next step is to communicate that openly with others. This can be difficult to do. Sharing your innermost beliefs, the beliefs you hold close to your heart, can put you in a vulnerable place. If you are rejected, you are truly rejected for who you are. But, then again, if you are rejected for being who you are, you are in a better place because you know you cannot be true to yourself with this person or in this environment. It is better to know that and move on than to pretend to be someone else and fake it. That is no fun at all. (It may be for a little while, but it gets old fast.)

The last part of authenticity is behaving ethically. If you behave according to your principles, you probably will behave ethically. If your principles are not exactly ethical, you may want to rethink them. When you are ethical, people trust you. When people trust you, they believe what you're saying to them and communication is much more straightforward. It is not easy to consistently behave ethically. No one ever said it was. You may not always feel like you are getting as much as you can when you behave ethically, but in the long run you will—and you will feel a lot better about yourself along the way.

Excerpt from CEO Jack Welch's Speech at His Final Operating Managers Meeting at GE

"I'd like to leave you some thoughts on ten things to reflect on as you go forward. This is not about nostalgia or memory lane. It's all about what's important tomorrow. It's about the future. First and foremost, integrity. This company and its people are all about integrity.

"I'm often asked, 'What worries you about GE, keeps you awake at night?' It is nothing about our businesses. It's just someone doing something stupid from a legal point, and bringing tarnish to the company, and destroying themselves and their families in the process. Never stop being diligent about it. Never leave anyone in the organization that works for you in doubt about where you stand on this subject. You can't talk about it too much.

"But integrity is a lot more than just legal stuff. It's a set of values that must guide all of us all the time. It's about always doing the right thing, not just the legal thing. Your employees, our employees, in every facet of their work lives, trust your integrity. Never, ever let them down" (Suseno 2010).

Authenticity is knowing who you are and what you value, communicating transparently with others, and behaving in accordance with your values. Behaving authentically is not always easy, but you ultimately feel better when you do. The section on authenticity in Chapter 3 and accompanying exercises in Part 3 will help you figure out who you are and deal with your imperfections. The exercises that accompany this chapter in Part 3 of the book will help you figure out what your values are and how to communicate openly about them and behave consistently with them.

CHAPTER 7

Foster Creativity

Why is creativity so important? Creativity and innovation are buzzwords in industry right now, but it is much bigger than that. Being creative is fundamental to getting by in REAL life. No matter how much planning we do, things change, pop up unexpectedly, and go wrong. REAL life is full of surprises, and we need to flex to deal with them. A couple weeks ago, I attended a presentation where the presenter suddenly could not continue. The host asked me on the spot if I could come up with something to engage the audience with for the next hour. I was surprised. I was flexible, and I was creative. I teamed up with a colleague, and we launched into an interactive discussion with the audience members to personalize the topic to each person in the room. It was a grand success, and we were both invigorated by the experience.

Just this morning, I went to get a coffee at the local coffee shop. The coffee grinder jammed, but that didn't stop the barista. He took the bin of coffee beans off of the smaller coffee grinder used for decaf coffee, punched a hole in the bottom of a paper cup, filled that with regular coffee beans, and put it on the decaf grinder. My coffee was barely delayed. In other words, you don't have to be a consultant to need creativity in your job.

In fact, you don't even have to be working to need creativity in REAL life. Being resourceful and able to improvise is critical to getting by day to day. When you're hungry and you only have five ingredients in the house, what can you make for a meal? When you're traveling and your luggage is lost, how do you dress yourself for the rest of your vacation? When you leave your textbook at school and have a test the next day, how do you study? To come up with creative solutions to problems, you need to be limber. You need to be flexible and resilient and have the free space in your brain to think. Creativity is not easy to learn and control. It comes and goes and is practical at times and utterly impractical at other times. Creativity has a mind of its own, and you have to be limber to foster it.

What Is Creativity?

Creativity is hard to describe. Many books have been written on the topic, just like many books have been written on how to be a great leader, but there is no single recipe for success. People are creative in different ways, and creativity takes on many forms. The most important thing about creativity, for our purposes, is that you can't force it. Creativity requires flexibility, and that is often not how we choose to live our lives. We tend to be very structured and scheduled these days, not to mention overstressed, and that is not the best way to foster creativity.

Creativity Is Unscheduled

Have you ever tried to have a creative idea on a schedule? It's like when someone tells you to say something funny. All your jokes and funny stories fly out the window. Your mind goes blank, and you say you can't be funny on command. Suddenly you are more serious than ever. Writer's or painter's block, staring at a blank page or canvas, is a problem that arises when we are trying to be creative on a schedule.

Creativity takes time—not just continuous time but time to let ideas sit, time to make connections, and time for connections to transform into conscious ideas. There is a reason for the cocktail napkin design and the back of the envelope calculation: creative people are thinking about things at all times of the day and night. Creativity doesn't happen on a schedule. Creativity doesn't exist only between the hours of nine and five. Most importantly, creativity does not go well with over-scheduling and multitasking.

"All great achievements require time."
—Maya Angelou

How do we make time to be creative? We need to build some downtime into our schedules. It means not filling up unutilized time with senseless chatter. Wait in line at the supermarket without texting a friend; just wait and let your mind wander. Wait at the doctor's office without playing a video game; just sit and let your mind wander. Drive to your destination without putting on your headset; just drive and let your mind wander. Prepare a meal without turning on the TV; just cook and let your mind wander. Take one less class, sign up for one less extracurricular activity, or schedule one less playdate. Just have time to relax and let your mind wander.

Creativity Is Unstructured

Have you ever noticed that the most creative people are often frustratingly difficult to deal with? Try making plans with them. They are late, or they decide they want to do something completely different from what you had planned. They are interested in seemingly inane things, like a paper bag or a stain on the sidewalk. But they have the most amazing ideas!

I have advised numerous doctoral candidates on how to write a dissertation. Invariably, the students get stuck. They have writer's block, or they lose their motivation, or they just can't think about what to do. I tell them to forget about writing and designing the most fabulous experiment of all time. Instead, go for a walk, sit in a café, go on a date, reorganize your files, or back up your hard drive. Do something—anything—to let your mind wander. Write when your mind is ready to write. Do something else when it is not. Don't make yourself miserable trying to write when you are not in the right state of mind. I give this advice to doctoral students because it works. When the creative moment does emerge, the students write and write and write, for hours at a time. (And their boyfriends, family members, or classmates get very annoyed at them for canceling plans they had!)

How do we meet deadlines on creative projects? There are three steps:

1. Give yourself enough time in your project plan for creativity to emerge.
2. Start early; don't procrastinate until the last minute. (Yes, some people are creative under pressure, and if that works for you, then use it. But generally creativity takes time.)
3. Set up a plan that is flexible. Find tasks you can do to set yourself up to be creative so when you are not in a creative mind-set, you will not lose time and delay your progress. For example, you may need to research your competition or what has already been done in the field in which you are working. Do that when you are not ready to produce. You may need to generate funds to pay for your project; do that when you are not in a creative mood. You may have other projects (or homework) that need to be done. Do them when you are not in a creative mood so when you are ready to be creative, you do not have other work that needs to be done.

Creativity Is Unquantifiable

Those of us in the business of assessment are constantly asked to measure people's creativity. We try, but it is very hard to do. Try defining creativity. That in itself is hard. Does an idea have to be useful? Does it have to be beautiful? Who judges creativity? Does it have to appeal to the masses? Should it be understood by only an elite few? As you can see, creativity is rather subjective. More importantly, whether creative ideas generate a large profit depends on a whole different set of factors, such as timing, marketing, investment, and so on.

"Every profound innovation is based on an inward-bound journey, and going to a deeper place where knowing comes to the surface."
—W. Brian Arthur, noted economist of the Santa Fe Institute

Different Types of Creativity

Are you someone who is very resourceful and great at improvising? Or are you an artist who paints fresh interpretations of landscapes? Creativity comes in many shapes and forms, and they are all valued in the workplace. Aesthetic creativity is important in advertising, industrial design, fashion design, cooking, architecture, and many different areas. It is less important to get the aesthetics right in accounting or heart surgery; function and accuracy are much more important in these contexts. Innovation is important in designing new products, such as in engineering toy development. Innovation also can be very useful in manufacturing (e.g., speeding up production) and business processes (e.g., streamlining 911 calls to emergency response units).

Improving products and processes is another form of creativity. For example, engineers at Sony didn't invent the television, but they greatly improved picture quality. Fostering creativity in others is also very important. A manager who encourages her team members to be creative, doesn't squelch ideas, and doesn't punish or humiliate team members for coming up with bad ideas is a manager who will foster creativity in her team. Even if she doesn't generate the ideas herself, she is a valuable creative resource for the company.

Reflection:

What kind(s) of creativity do you have? Think about the different contexts in which you stand out as having "unique" or "helpful"

or "good" or "creative" outputs. Contexts could include: home, work, school, recreation, entertainment, emergencies, problems, alone, in groups, with friends, with strangers, fiction, reality, happy, sad, and so on.

Creativity Is Failure

"I am not judged by the number of times I fail, but by the number of times I succeed; and the number of times I succeed is in direct proportion to the number of times I can fail and keep on trying."
—Tom Hopkins

Twelve publishers rejected J. K. Rowling's original Harry Potter novel before it was published by Bloomsbury. Walt Disney bankrupted his first several businesses. Thomas Edison invented thousands of lightbulbs before he invented one that worked. Vincent van Gogh sold only one painting in his entire life, and it was to a friend. The most creative ideas tend to come from failure because people learn what does not work and develop what does.

How do we fail to create? Resilience is the key. We need to be strong enough to take the risk, fail, and get back up and try again—over and over again—until we get a good result. It may take hours, days, weeks, and even years. We need to have the drive, focus, curiosity, and tenacity to hang in there.

Reflection:

Think about a time when you created something that you were very proud of. What led up to that creation? How many times did you fail in the process? How did you feel during the period from when you started to when you succeeded? Did you give up in the process? If so, what did you do to recover? What kept you going until you succeeded?

Creativity Is Asking Questions

"Successful people ask better questions, and as a result, they get better answers."
—Anthony Robbins

In the workplace it is fairly easy to find leaders with strong advocacy and influencing skills, but it is harder to find good leaders with strong listening and inquiry skills. These skills are key to successful communications and are critical to generating creativity. Listening to find out what someone's needs are helps you come up with better solutions for them. Asking probing questions helps get at what needs must be met and what is not working. Asking questions helps people think more deeply about things and go to a place where new ideas are put forth.

Reflection:

Look at the following questions that people asked to lead to creative and innovative solutions. If you are not familiar with any of these examples, look them up. What questions do you have? Keep a journal, and write them down as they come to you.

"What would the universe look like if I were riding on the end of a light beam at the speed of light?"
—Einstein, "Theory of Relativity"

"What is the most ethical action we can take?"
—James Burke, Johnson & Johnson CEO, 1980s Tylenol crisis

"Where can I get a good hamburger on the road?"
—Ray Kroc, McDonald's

Being Limber Fosters Creativity

REAL Life

Resilient
Empowered
Authentic
Limber

Creativity is hard to define, but it most certainly involves having a limber mind and constitution. It's a stretch to "think outside the box." It requires flexibility to work on an unstructured schedule. It requires resilience to bounce back from failure. It requires agility to respond to new information. All of this is necessary to succeeding in REAL life. The exercises in Part 3 will help you limber up your mind to foster creativity.

CHAPTER 8

What's Next?

"Leadership, like swimming, cannot be learned by reading about it."
—Henry Mintzberg

My goal is to help young people be better prepared for work and life—to help them be self-sufficient, productive members of our society—and to encourage parents to let go and count on the kids to figure it out. In this book, I've offered practical solutions for parents, educators, and managers to prepare youth for the workplace. I presented a model for success in REAL life that focuses on being resilient, empowered, authentic, and limber. I offered five critical actions to take to succeed in work and life: (1) accept imperfection, (2) build resilience, (3) develop independence, (4) polish communication skills, and (5) foster creativity. In Part 3, I present exercises to help you take the next step in your development if you so choose. But that's not what you may want to do right now. You might prefer to engage in discussion with others about these issues, reflect on what you've read, or put the book on the shelf and forget about it. I hope you don't do the latter. Rather, I hope you are inspired to help yourself and others be successful in REAL life.

REAL Life

Resilient
Empowered
Authentic
Limber

What Will You Do Now?

What struck you the most in the previous chapters? What will you do with it? My suggestion is to turn to Part 3 and start with the reflection questions on that topic. See the figure below for an example of an exercise taken from Chapter 1. After you have thought about the issue, it's time to take action. Action steps follow the reflection questions in Part 3. They range in size and scale. You can choose how big a step you want to take. The example below involves getting input from other people. That would be a moderate action because it takes time and effort to schedule time with others and ask them to engage with you. A small action would be something you could do on your own, like write a development plan (Action 2 for Chapter 1). A larger action would be to practice specific active listening skills during interactions with others. This requires you to put a new tool to use in a real situation.

Sample Exercises from Part 3

Reflection on What You Need at Work:

1. **Go through *Table 1: Common Success Factors at Work,* and choose the success factors that seem important to where you want to go as a leader. Think about how you behave and select one or two success factors you think are your strengths. Pick one or two you think you would benefit from developing. Think about ways you can leverage your strengths and develop your gaps in the activities you have going on right now.**

Action for What You Need at Work:

1. **If you are not sure what success factors are important in the type of work you do (or want to do), ask. Find one or two people in that field who will make time for**

you, and ask them to go through the table of success factors with you and highlight the factors that are most important.

What Else Is There to Think About?

Many aspects of the issues I brought up are outside of your control. For example, if you are a teacher, you can't control what goes on inside your students' homes. Conversely, if you are a parent, you can't control what your kids do when they go to school. You may not have control over these situations, but you might have influence. For example, you can be a role model by sharing a mistake that you made, how you felt, and how you handled it. When the child faces a setback, she or he may recall how you dealt with yours and be motivated to get through it. In other words, it is about outfitting kids with the tools they need to be successful. They ultimately have to choose to use them on their own.

You may have noticed that the core principle is "let go." This principle holds for both sides of the equation—for caregivers and for youth. Caregivers: Leave it to the military to protect and serve. What parents and educators need to do is to nurture and teach, not do it for them. We don't need to build bigger and bigger walls around our children to keep them from danger. It just makes danger that much more enticing. We need to teach children how to avoid danger and what to do when they encounter it—because they inevitably will. We don't want to leave them empty-handed so they cannot cope without an adult around to save them.

Youth: Step up to the plate, and try it on your own. Go to parents, teachers, and managers for guidance and advice if you are stuck. But don't go to them first for instructions, and don't be afraid to make mistakes and learn from them. The assistant dean of a prominent business school told me just the other day that he learned what kinds of executive education classes worked well in his region. How do you think he learned? He tried classes that didn't work and learned why. He tried some more and did better. It took years to get it right, but now it is a thriving program. He told me this story as he made the decision to try a course offering that had failed twice in the past. He knows it is an important course and wants to figure out how to get it right. This is how successful people work; they try till they get it right.

What Am I Going to Do?

As a matter of fact, I am trying till I get it right too. This book underwent some changes before it was ready to publish. My next book, even more. But I'd like to tell you about it, because I'm going to keep working on it till I get it right.

My next book addresses the reasons that we need *this* book. It is a social commentary on why we are in the predicament where people aren't as prepared as they need to be for life and work. How has parenting changed? Why has it changed? Why have schools changed? How are we different from other societies? Why? How has the workplace changed over the last several decades? Why? What are we doing to make conscious change? What are we doing inadvertently to create change that we don't want? What are the side effects of changes that we do want? What are we missing in our awareness of the world?

In short, my next book is a social commentary that challenges the direction we've taken in parenting and educating youth. I discuss the consequences of overprotecting, overstructuring, and expecting perfection and explore how we got to this point.

Spread the Word

My goal is help young people be self-sufficient, productive members of our society and to encourage parents to let go and count on the kids to figure it out. I blog and speak regularly about these issues. I invite you to keep in touch with me online and engage with me and with others to continue the dialogue and to inspire people to take action. Talk to individual parents and youth. Talk to educators and political leaders. Talk to organizations that are employing youth. Spread the word. Ask questions. Think.

This book gives specific advice to parents, educators, managers, and youth to help prepare young people for the rigors of adult life. But the implications of this book are far greater. Imagine a generation of leaders who are living with their parents, who look to others to tell them what the next step is, who fall apart when they make a mistake or someone criticizes them, and who don't feel comfortable interacting with their team face-to-face. How prominent will our society be? How innovative will our industries be? How strong will our economy be?

These issues affect all of us, not just parents and their kids. This is a societal issue that could bring our society down. We live in a Darwinian world of the survival of the fittest. To compete in this world, we have to be not only smart but tough and resourceful. We have to band together as a society to support each other. We have to be able to interact with other societies in a constructive way to share limited resources and maintain peace. It's a lot to do. It's of critical importance to all of us to prepare the next generation of leaders and members of our society to be able to handle what they have to do.

"It is our job to prepare our children for the road, not prepare the road for our children."
—Dr. Wendy Mogel

PART 3
Exercises

Chapter 1: What Is Going On at Work?

Getting Help

Reflection:

1. How much do you depend on others? When do you ask for help? How preprogrammed is it for you to ask someone to do something for you?
    a. Ask someone to hold your purse/package/coat while you are putting on your shoes.
    b. Ask the waiter what to order.
    c. Ask the teacher to send you the homework assignment because you did not write it down or you lost it.
    d. Rely on your parents to wake you up in the morning.
    e. Make your own breakfast/lunch/dinner.
2. How much frustration do you experience? How do you handle it?

Action:

1. Try doing things on your own.
2. We often give up or ask for help to avoid feeling frustrated. While frustration is not an enjoyable feeling, it does help us solve problems. Next time you are feeling frustrated, work through your frustration. It might be best to start when you are alone. That way, you can actually be frustrated and get through it. Once you have done this a few times, it will help you realize you can get through it on your own. The next step will be to work on managing your frustration so you don't alienate others. See Chapter 4, Build Resilience, for ideas on that.

Communication and Relationships

Reflection:

1. What is your preferred method of communicating (chat, e-mail, face-to-face, telephone, etc.)?
2. What is the preferred method of communicating of the top ten people with whom you communicate?
3. How much do you vary your method of communication depending on whom you are communicating with?
4. How comfortable are you communicating in each of the following ways?
   a. Face-to-face
   b. Telephone (voice)
   c. Video
   d. E-mail
   e. Chat/IM/text
5. What does "friend" mean to you?
6. What are you willing to do for your friends? Family? Colleagues?
7. What are your friends/family/colleagues willing to do for you?

Action:

1. Set up some face-to-face time with the people who are important to you and with people with whom you would like to build better relationships.
   a. Suggestions for adults: get lunch, coffee, or a beer; swing by their office; get tickets to a game or event; or set up a playdate or activity for the kids.
   b. Suggestions for youth: go together to a school event; get ice cream or a Frappuccino; get tickets to a game or other event; go shopping; hang out; study together; or carpool.
   c. If these are lame, come up with your own ideas!

2. Offer to do favors for others. In networking, this is the first principle. Many people think networking is about asking people to do things for them, but the best networkers offer to do things for others first. Later, the others will owe them a favor. In building relationships, it is the same thing. You invite someone to your house for dinner, and they will feel obligated to return the invitation. Even if people do not return the favors per se, they still have a positive feeling toward you, and that is important. They are probably indirectly returning them by saying nice things about you to others.

Preferred Environment

Reflection:

1. What do you feel you need to be able to get your work done? Everybody needs something. The question becomes, how much do you really need versus want?
2. Consider the following attributes of a work environment, and think about what suits your work style best. There is no right or wrong choice to any of these.
    a. Competition versus praise
    b. Teamwork versus autonomy
    c. Supervision versus independence
    d. Fun versus serious
    e. Action versus analytical thinking
    f. Fast pace versus time to be thorough
    g. Make money versus do good
    h. Intense work schedule versus balanced life
    i. Lavish resources versus focus on work
    j. Prestige versus job well done

Action:

1. Take a work style assessment, such as the Myers-Briggs Type Inventory or the Keirsey Temperament Sorter. I highly recommend the Birkman Method (www.birkman.com) for a more complete experience. This will help you figure out what kind of work environment best suits you. The Birkman Method instrument, for example, identifies your preferred ways of working and being in all sorts of areas, such as how many people you are comfortable working with, how directly or indirectly you like to communicate with people and have them communicate with you, and what levels of competition and congeniality you work best in. There are many instruments out there that will help you figure out what environment you thrive in.

Entitlement

Reflection:

1. Be honest with yourself. How entitled are you? What do you feel that you deserve to get without putting anything out there?
2. How does your entitlement compare to others around you? People of your own age? Older and younger people? People from other backgrounds?
3. How does your entitlement compare to others in remote places? For example, think about the people in this world who wake up in the morning needing to look for clean water to drink and food to eat. How does that influence what you think you deserve?

Action:

1. Travel. Expose yourself to other cultures and other levels of socioeconomic status. Find out what other people have, what they take for granted, and how content they are with what they have. Likely, you will find out you have a lot more than most others in this world. Whenever I travel overseas, the thing I am happiest about when I return is the American bathroom—flush toilets, soft toilet paper, hot showers, space to move around, and cleanliness. It may sound crazy, but if you get around enough you will surely agree. You do not need to leave the country to do this. You probably do not even have to leave the city you live in to fully appreciate what you have.
2. Take an inventory of your stuff, and see how much of it you use. Get rid of the extra.
3. Try going without your comforts for a week, and figure out which ones are most important. I have discovered my most important luxury is a hot, frothy mocha. Can I live without it? Of course. But it is a luxury I really enjoy and treat myself to when it is available. If not, I will appreciate a hot cup of tea or coffee, or get by on nothing at all. Which of your comforts are luxuries? What can you live without and still be comfortable?

Chapter 2: What You Need at Work

Success Factors at Work

Reflection:

1. Go through *Table 1: Common Success Factors at Work,* and choose the success factors that seem important to where you

want to go as a leader. Think about how you behave, and select one or two success factors you think are your strengths. Pick one or two you think you would benefit from developing. Think about ways you can leverage your strengths and develop your gaps in the activities you have going on right now.

Action:

1. If you are not sure what success factors are important in the type of work you do (or want to do), ask. Find one or two people in that field who will make time for you, and ask them to go through the table of success factors with you and highlight the factors that are most important.
2. Create a development plan for yourself that includes one or two success factors to leverage and one or two success factors to develop. Use the format below or create your own. Once you have chosen the success factors, figure out some specific actions you can take to leverage and develop them. Make yourself accountable by including a due date and the resources and people you will need to involve.

Development Plan
Strengths
1. 2. 3.
Development Opportunities
1. 2. 3.

Development Plan		
Action Plan		
Action	**Target Date**	**Resources/People to Involve**
1.		
2.		
3.		
4.		
5.		

Real Life at Work

Reflection:

1. Take the ExecuStart Self-Assessment below. Answer honestly. When you have completed it, go back through it and think about what you can do to increase the frequency of behaviors you do not do very often.

ExecuStart Self-Assessment Qualities for Success in Life			
	Rarely	**Sometimes**	**Most of the Time**
Personal Power			
1. **I have a strong sense of who I am.**			
2. **When I make decisions, I am grounded in purpose and values.**			
3. **My head, heart, and body are integrated, and my behaviors and decisions incorporate all three.**			
4. **I have the courage to act on my convictions.**			
5. **I take the initiative to get things done on my own.**			
6. **I have the self-discipline to control myself.**			

ExecuStart Self-Assessment Qualities for Success in Life			
	Rarely	Sometimes	Most of the Time
Resilience 1. I take risks to expand my horizons. 2. I am willing to fail to learn. 3. I have a "can do" attitude. 4. I have long-term goals worth working for. 5. I have a network of people who support me when I need it. 6. I have a positive outlook on life.			
Creativity and Renewal 1. I am curious. 2. I embrace innovation and change. 3. I am aware of what is going on around me. 4. I respond to changing signals around me. 5. I willingly let go of control. 6. I am committed to a lifetime of learning.			
Connection with Others 1. People listen to what I have to say and notice when I'm not there. 2. I have an open heart and mind to new and different people and situations. 3. People tell me I'm a good listener. 4. I advocate for myself to get what I want. 5. I am good at getting people to agree with me. 6. I genuinely appreciate diversity in all its forms.			

ExecuStart Self-Assessment Qualities for Success in Life			
	Rarely	**Sometimes**	**Most of the Time**
Integrity 1. **I do what is right, even if it is not easy.** 2. **I am clear about what my personal values are.** 3. **I know what is important to me.** 4. **I respect others.** 5. **My actions are consistent with my beliefs.** 6. **I am accountable for my actions and mistakes.**			
Wisdom 1. **I seek the knowledge and experience of others.** 2. **I am humble; I don't expect to know the most.** 3. **I learn from life's experiences—both successes and failures.** 4. **I show appreciation and gratitude.** 5. **I easily recognize the connected nature of things.**			

Action:

1. Choose one or two of the behaviors you identified from the ExecuStart Self-Assessment, and find a situation (or situations) where you can implement them. Check in with yourself after the situation(s) to see how it went. Think about what you could have done differently. Imagine yourself doing it differently, and try it that way next time.
2. Look for opportunities to work with people who exhibit strength in the qualities you want to improve. Observe what they do well, and find a way to incorporate some of those

behaviors into your way of doing things. Make sure what you do fits with who you are. What works for one person might not work for another.

3. Complete a development plan (see above) for the ExecuStart qualities you identified.

Chapter 3: Accept Imperfection

Reflection:

1. What does "perfect" mean to you? For yourself? For your children? For your spouse?
2. Who determines what perfection is? You? Your parents? Your neighbors? College admissions officers?
3. How perfect do you have to be?
4. How perfect does your child have to be?
5. How perfect are you?
6. How perfect is your parent/child?
7. What happens when you see that you (or your child) are less than perfect?
8. How authentic are you? In other words, to what extent do you hide your imperfections from others?

Action:

1. Be a role model by sharing your imperfections. Use real opportunities to model imperfections in the moment, and also set yourself up from time to time to show your kids you can recover gracefully. Lose a game, spill something, trip over a toy, do or say something naughty, and apologize.
2. Look for role models for you to follow. Observe people who are gracefully imperfect, who do not apologize for being less than spectacular. Learn from them.

3. Figure out what is driving your need for perfection (if you have one). Was this the only way to get attention from your parents? Or to not get punished? Are you overcompensating for something else? Are you hypercompetitive? If so, why? Perhaps you used perfectionism as a coping mechanism for something at one point in your life that is no longer present. Figure out what is driving this need, and then figure out how to lay off a bit and appreciate yourself (and others) for who you (they) really are.

Being Authentic

Reflection:

1. Read and reflect on the following poem.

We Never Know Who We Are
By Meg Wheatley (Wheatley and Frieze 2011)

We never know who we are
(this is strange, isn't it?)
or what vows we made
or who we knew
or what we hoped for
or where we were
when this world's dreams
were seeded.

Until the day just one of us

sighs a gentle longing
and we all feel the change
one of us calls our name
and we all know to be there

one of us tells a dream
and we all breathe life into it

one of us asks "why?"
and we all know the answer.

It is very strange. We never know who we are.

2. List the values that are important to your life (and parenting). After you have completed your list, go back and rank them in the order of their importance to you.
    a. Which values are nonnegotiable?
    b. Which values are desirable but not mandatory?
    c. Which values depend on the situation?
3. Do any of your values conflict with each other? What will you do when there is a conflict between your values?
4. Recall a situation in which your values were tested under pressure, where you may have deviated. How much did you behave according to your values at that time? Why or why not? What forces caused you to deviate? If you had a "do over," what would you do differently?

Chapter 4: Build Resilience

Reflection:

1. Describe someone who you think is particularly resilient. How do they behave in tough situations? Are they calm? Do they use their sense of humor? Do they become energized? What aspects of their behavior can you use?
2. When are you most/least resilient? In the moment? With big issues? With other people around? What can you take from the times you are more resilient to the times are less resilient?

3. How do you calm yourself down? How can you apply this method to situations when you lose your calm?
4. Describe someone who you think is particularly grounded. What makes them grounded? What do they do to stay grounded?
5. What kind of person do you want to be? How far are you from being that person? What can you do to get closer to being that person?
6. How can you move out of the victim role to take situations into your own hands? Do you find yourself feeling like a victim a lot? If so, how are you letting yourself be victimized? Are you particularly sensitive about this subject? Does the person know you are feeling attacked? How can you communicate this? What can you do to change the dynamic?

Action:

1. For parents: Use the "guided self-correction" process to help your child correct his or her own behavior after making a mistake (Josephson et al. 2001). When something goes wrong, ask your child general questions to find out what it was and then more specific questions to help them think through what they need to do to make it right. Make sure not to answer the questions for them. Questions might take the form of
   a. What happened?
   b. Why do you think the person (e.g., coach, boss) reacted that way?
   c. What would you have done if you were in his/her position?
   d. What can you do now that might make things better?
   e. What would be a positive solution to this problem?
2. To maintain a high level of integrity, make promises only if you plan to keep them.

3. To avoid being bullied, take an inventory of your boundaries, write them down, and have a response for when they have been breached. For example, if you've decided that you don't do homework for other people, you can make that your policy. When someone tries to bully you into doing their homework for them, you can matter-of-factly say that you don't do that, rather than engaging in a dialogue that will leave you doing something you don't feel comfortable doing.
4. The nothing moment: Try doing nothing. Space out. See what comes to mind. Let yourself be bored. Put the phone away. No texts. No games. No Facebook.
    a. Look around you. What do you see? Look again. What else do you see?
    b. Is there dirt on the street? How did it get there?
    c. Are people talking to each other at a nearby table? What are they saying? What aren't they saying? How do they know each other? What are their personal histories?
    d. Is the wind blowing? Where did it come from?
    e. How are you feeling? How is the environment affecting how you are feeling? How are other things affecting the way you are feeling? How is this exercise affecting the way you are feeling?
    f. Is there something that you need to think about? Why not think about it now? Truly think about it. What haven't you considered before? How does how you are feeling right now change your perspective?

Chapter 5: Develop Independence

For Parents

Reflection:

1. How independent are your children right now? How independent do you want them to be? If you want them to be more independent than they are, what or who is holding them back?
2. What contributes to your fear of letting your children be more independent? What stems from the unknown versus the known? What can you find out to help you reduce your fear?
3. What is the most courageous thing you have ever done? What drove you to do it?
4. How trusting are you? What contributed to this in your past? What contributes to it now?
5. How much do you trust your children? What would it take to trust them more?

Action:

1. Examine your news sources, and determine how much they are contributing to your fears. Consider changing your news sources to get more accurate accounts of safety and dangers in your area.
2. Listen carefully when your friends and colleagues talk or gossip about the latest tragedy or scandal. How much of a concern is it to you and your family, really? What can you learn from this to avoid getting into this situation? What precautions can you take?

3. Write down a list of capabilities you think your kids should have to be able to take care of themselves. Start teaching your kids these skills. Some of the skills might include: cleaning, cooking, sewing, home repair, budgeting, self-defense, and decision making.
4. Give your kids opportunities to earn your trust in the form of responsibilities around the house. For example, if a kid can complete a chore regularly, on time, without being reminded, he or she may be ready to handle homework on his or her own.

For Youth

Reflection:

1. How independent are you right now? How independent do you want to be? If you want to be more independent than you are, what or who is holding you back?
2. Do your parents know your level of capability? What capabilities do you have that they might be unaware of? For example, can you cook yourself a meal?
3. What capabilities would you like to develop to allow yourself greater independence? For example, learn how to use the public transportation system in your area.
4. How much work are you willing to put in to be more independent? For example, get a job to pay for your own stuff.

Action:

1. Read the book *Right Risk* by Bill Treasurer (Treasurer 2003) to learn how to take the risk of trying new things in a safe way.
2. Write down your goals. If you know where you want to be, you can figure out what you need to do to get there. Having

an end goal can help you get through the discomfort of trying something new.

3. Instead of fighting fear, make it work for you. Fear gives you energy that you can rechannel in the direction you want to go. For example, turn your fear into excitement, exhilaration, speed, or animation. Find a situation in which you can put this principle into action.
4. Ask your parents what kinds of things they did for themselves when they were your age. Ask them to teach you how to do them too.

Chapter 6: Polish Communication Skills

Reflection:

1. Whom do you admire for their ability to communicate effectively? What do they do that you admire?
2. How do they make you feel? Do you feel heard? How?
3. Describe a situation in which you felt the communication went terribly. What happened? With whom were you communicating? How did you feel as a communicator and as a recipient of communication? What was missing? What could you have done to turn things around? What could you have done to help it go more smoothly from the start? What would you like to have gotten from the other person? What could you do to try to get that?

Action:

1. Ground yourself before an interaction with others using the following exercise. Grounding can be a foundation for effective interaction. When you are grounded, you are better able to stay calm and focused on the present. Your presence is

conveyed to others, and it encourages a reciprocal presence, making the interaction less muddled and more satisfying.

Grounding Exercise Adapted from Stan Herman

Before an important meeting or presentation, or any time you feel pressured, find a quiet space, sit down, and go through the following grounding process:

- **Close your eyes (or leave them half open if you'd rather), and loosen any tight clothing.**
- **Feel your feet on the floor and your buttocks on the chair. Keep your spine straight and relaxed, shoulders and head level.**
- **Patiently, one area at a time, check your body for tensions. Start at your feet and go all the way up to your head—feet, ankles, lower legs, upper legs, buttocks, abdomen, chest, back, hands, arms, shoulders, neck, jaw, face, and scalp (or whole head at once). Wherever you find tension, intensify it for a few moments, and then let it go using the following tension release process.**
- **Breathe in deeply, tighten the muscles *as hard as you can* for five seconds, and then allow the muscles to relax while slowly exhaling.**
- **If you have time (about ten minutes), go through the tension release process for your entire body. You may have tensions you didn't realize.**
- **Don't forget to breathe!**
- **After you've checked the top of your head, go back for a moment to feeling the ground under your feet again and the chair under your buttocks. Notice how you feel overall. Remind yourself of your presence by thinking (or saying aloud), *Here I am.***

Now it's time to get down to business.

2. Practice active listening using the LAR model in the chapter. Find a partner to practice with. Choose a topic on which to give each other feedback, such as how well the person listens or how she could improve her swing. Person A will give feedback, and person B will listen actively. After you have finished, talk about what it felt like with each other to give feedback and to listen actively. Then switch roles and do it again.
3. Get feedback from others. Do a mini-assessment of yourself, and get others to assess you too. Write up questions that you have about how well you communicate, such as "How well do I listen?" Make a scale, such as one to five. Rate yourself. Be honest. Ask a few trusted friends or colleagues to rate you honestly too. Use it as a jumping-off point for discussion on how you could improve. Be prepared to receive honest feedback before you do this though. Try grounding yourself beforehand.

Trust

Reflection:

1. Take the following Trust Inventory to bring awareness to yourself about how trustworthy you appear to yourself and others. Be honest with yourself. When you are done, go back and think about behaviors you might want to change to increase your trustworthiness.

Trust Inventory

For each item, rate on the scale using a number from 1 to 5:

1 = Strongly Disagree ⟵⟶ Strongly Agree = 5

Rate each item twice. Rate the items from the perspective of:

- Self: how would you rate yourself?
- Other: how would you anticipate another person would rate you?

	Trust Inventory	Self	Other
	Integrity and Intention		
1.	**Acts with honesty and integrity**		
2.	**Is not self-promoting**		
3.	**Stands up for values when actions of the senior leadership/organization are inconsistent with them**		
4.	**Takes into account my interests and needs, as well as those of the organization**		
5.	**Allows others to speak openly without fear of negative consequences**		
6.	**Tells the truth, not just what people want to hear**		
7.	**Doesn't shy away from conflict**		
8.	**Genuinely cares about other people and is concerned about their well-being**		
	Capabilities and Results		
9.	**Is sought after by many people for opinions**		
10.	**Has knowledge and skills that make an important contribution to the team**		
11.	**Upgrades and increases knowledge and skills in all the important areas to stay relevant**		
12.	**Has the skill to effectively establish and rebuild trust**		

Trust Inventory	Self	Other
13. **Holds his/her team members accountable for deliverables**		
14. **Has a track record of success**		
15. **Takes responsibility for results; does not blame others**		

Action:

1. Creating team or group expectations: You can build trust in a team or group (as small as two people) by setting expectations of behavior right up front. If you are working with others, try pausing for a moment to discuss all your expectations around the following areas.

Team Issues	Areas to Explore
Timeliness	What are our expectations about responding to each other in a timely manner? How quickly do we expect people to get back to us?
Deadlines	What rules will we follow for adhering to deadlines? How should we warn each other when there are problems that may impact deadlines?
Coordination	To what extent are team members expected to coordinate on what's happening? How are we going to align with individual team members and as a whole?
Disagreement and conflict	Collaborative efforts are likely to have genuine differences of opinion, as well as misunderstandings. To keep solid working relationships intact, what are our expectations about how to surface problems and deal with conflict between individuals?
Recognition	One of the important ways to make teamwork satisfying is to make sure individuals are recognized and appreciated, as well as the entire team. To keep members motivated, what habits do we want to develop to acknowledge each other for ideas, contributions, and follow-through?

Emotions

Reflection:

1. How emotional are you? Do you display emotions often? Do you suppress your emotions often?
2. Do you control your emotions, or do your emotions control you? Or is it a bit of both? Think about the different situations in which you feel out of control. Why? What is triggering them? What could you do to maintain control?

Action:

1. Take an emotional intelligence assessment to find out what level of emotional intelligence you currently have. TalentSmart offers a quick and inexpensive online assessment you can access directly. Other assessment tools are available too, such as the EQ-i and the MSCEIT. You will need to contact someone with more experience to give you access to those instruments and a full debriefing to fully benefit from the experience.
2. Increase your ability to understand how your behaviors impact others. Check in with people you know to better understand their feelings and emotions in response to your actions.
3. Use what skills you already have in emotional intelligence to become more comfortable openly discussing emotions. Find a role model who is comfortable discussing emotions, and learn from him or her. Practice talking about emotions in safe situations to see how it feels.

Authenticity

Reflection:

1. Complete the Authentic Behavior Worksheet, below, which is based on work from George and Sims (2007). Think about what kinds of behaviors you want to do to behave more authentically. Read George and Sims' book for further reflection.

Authentic Behavior Worksheet:
Values, Behavioral Principles, and Ethical Boundaries

Values: The relative importance of the things that matter in your life.

Behavioral Principles: A set of standards to behave by, derived from your values. Principles are values translated into action.

Ethical Boundaries: The limits placed on your actions, based on your standards of ethical behavior.

Exercise:

1. List three values that are important to your life and the way you want to be. After you have done so, go back and rank them in the order of their importance to you.

Values	Rank
•	
•	
•	

2. List three behavioral principles you use (or want to use) in living your life. Then go back and rank-order them depending on which are most important to you.

Principles	Rank
• • •	

3. List three ethical boundaries you will not cross. Then rank-order them in terms of their importance to you.

Ethical Boundaries	Rank
• • •	

Action:

1. Put the behaviors from the Authentic Behavior Worksheet into action over the next week. Choose a situation (or situations) where you can implement the behaviors you want to do. Check in with yourself after the situation(s) to see how well you behaved according to your principles and values. Think about what you could have done differently to adhere more closely to them. Imagine yourself doing them, and put them in your mind for next time. Or go back and continue the situation with your new mindset, and see if you can improve the outcome. To do that, you may want to tell the person(s) with whom you interacted that it didn't turn out the way you had hoped and you would like to add something or have a redo. Be authentic about it.

Chapter 7: Foster Creativity

Creativity

Reflection:

1. What kind of creative person are you? Are you someone who likes to invent things? Are you better at building upon other people's ideas and making them better? Do you have a particular talent as a writer, musician, actor, or artist? Are you a free thinker, or do you prefer to solve problems? Are you resourceful? Are you good at leading a team of people to a creative solution? These are all different forms of creativity. We all have some amount of creativity in ourselves. Find what kind of creativity you have a passion for, and use it.

Action:

1. Instead of turning to an electronic device to keep you occupied, use your imagination to come up with something to do on your own.
2. Keep a notepad, diary, or electronic notepad with you to write down ideas as you have them. Write down your ideas, no matter how small or crazy they might seem. Go back and look through them periodically.
3. Do something creative for a hobby, like paint, fix up old cars, play a musical instrument, write poetry, sew, cook, garden, make jewelry, or take photographs. See how it makes you feel to be in the moment, to feel the creative juices flowing, to not be following someone else's instructions, to be adding your own flair. Carry this feeling over to other times when you could use a bit of creativity.

REFERENCES

Alsop, R. (2008). *The Trophy Kids Grow Up: How the Millennial Generations Is Shaking up the Workplace.* San Francisco, CA: Jossey-Bass.

Atlas, J. (2011). Super People. *New York Times.* Retrieved from http://www.nytimes.com/2011/10/02/opinion/sunday/meet-the-new-super-people.html?pagewanted=all&_r=0

Barford, I. N., & Hester, P. T. (2011). *Analysis of Generation Y Workforce Motivation Using Multiattribute Utility Theory.* Fort Belvoir, VA: Defense Acquisition University.

Belkin, L. (2007). Parents Who Can't Resist Smoothing Life's Bumps. *New York Times.* Retrieved from http://www.nytimes.com/2007/02/11/business/yourmoney/11wcol.html?_r=0

Belkin, L. (2010). The Way We Live Now: Living to Be a Parent. *New York Times Magazine.*

Blanchard, K., & Ridge, G. (2009). *Helping People Win at Work: A Business Philosophy Called "Don't Mark My Paper, Help Me Get an A".* Upper Saddle River, NJ: FT Press.

Bolles, R. N. (1990). *What Color Is Your Parachute? A Practical Manual for Job Hunters and Career Changers* (1990 ed.). Berkeley, CA: Ten Speed Press.

Brooks, R., & Goldstein, S. (2001). *Raising Resilient Children.* New York, NY: McGraw-Hill.

Byatzis, R., & McKee, A. (2005). *Resonant Leadership: Renewing Yourself and Connecting with Others Through Mindfulness, Hope, and Compassion.* Boston, MA: Harvard Business School Press.

Covey, S. M. R. (2006). *The Speed of Trust: The One Thing that Changes Everything.* New York, NY: Free Press.

Deresiewicz, W. (2014). Don't Send Your Kid to the Ivy League. The nations top colleges are turning our kids into zombies. *The New Republic.*

Djordjevic, A. (2010). *Factors mediating the effect of age on early career burnout.* ((C-level) psychology (2PS013)), Royal Caroline Institute, Sweden.

Duckworth, A., Peterson, C., Mathews, M., & Kelly, D. (2007). Grit: Perseverance and Passion for Long-Term Goals. *Journal of Personality and Social Psychology,* 92(6), 1087–1101.

Edmondson, A. C. (2011). Strategies for Learning from Failure. *Harvard Business Review,* 49-55.

Engel, S., & Sandstrom, M. (2010). There's Only One Way to Stop a Bully. *The New York Times.*

Faw, L. (2011). Why Millennial Women Are Burning Out at Work By 30.

Fisher, A. (2009). When Gen X Runs the Show. *Time Magazine, 173,* 48-49.

Fred, D. (2010). Understanding Engineers in the Generation Y. *The Engineering Daily.net.*

George, B., & Sims, P. (2007). *True North: Discover your Authentic Leadership.* San Francisco, CA: Josey-Bass.

Hepplewhite, P. (2001). *Words Along Wires: The Story of Alexander Graham Bell* (pp. 34-35). Great Britain: Hodder Wayland.

Hira, N. A. (2007). You Raised Them, Now Manage Them. *Fortune,* 38-46.

Icahn, C. (2011). Why Blockbuster Failed. *Harvard Business Review.*

Ignatius, A. (2011). When We Fail at Failure. *Harvard Business Review.*

Isaacson, W. (2011). *Steve Jobs.* New York, NY: Knopf Doubleday Publishing Group.

Jager-Hyman, J. (2009). Where You Go To College Doesn't Matter. *Forbes.*

Jobs, S. (2005). 'You've got to find what you love,' Jobs says. *Stanford Report.* Retrieved from: http://news.stanford.edu/news/2005/june15/jobs-061505.html

Josephson, M. S., Peter, V. J., & Dowd, T. (2001). *Parenting to Build Character in Your Teen.* Boys Town Nebraska: Boys Town Press.

Khidekel, M. (2010). Career Burnout: Maya Luz. *Marie Claire.*

Kim, H., Knight, D. K., & Crutsinger, C. (2009). Generation Y employees' retail work experience: The mediating effect of job characteristics. *Journal of Business Research, 62,* 548–556.

KIPP Foundation. "Character Counts." Retrieved October 5, 2013, 2013, from http://www.kipp.org/our-approach/character

Kolker, R. (2012). Cheating Upwards.Stuyvesant kids do it. Harvard kids do it. Smart kids may especially do it. But why? *New York Magazine.*

Kramer, R. M. (2009). Rethinking Trust. *Harvard Business Review* (June, 2009), 69-77.

Larson, D. W. (2004). Distrust: Prudent, If Not Always Wise. In R. Hardin (Ed.), *Distrust* (pp. 34-59). New York, NY: Russell Sage Foundation.

Levine, M. (2006). *The Price of Privilege.* New York, NY: HarperCollins Publishers.

Liker, J. K., & Hoseus, M. (2008). *Toyota Culture: The Heart and Soul of the Toyota Way.* New York, NY: McGraw Hill.

Manson, Bill. (May 27, 2009). You're Standing Right Next to Me but You're Not There. *San Diego Reader,* pp. 25-42.

Mayer, J. D., & Salovey, P. (1997). What Is Emotional Intelligence? In P. Salovey & D. Sluyter (Eds.), *Emotional Development and Emotional Intelligence: Educational Implications* (pp. 3-31). New York, NY: Basic Books.

Meister, J. C., & Willyerd, K. (2010). *The 2020 Workplace: How Innovative Companies Attract, Develop, and Keep Tomorrow's Employees Today.* New York, NY: HarperCollins.

Meister, J. (2012). Job Hopping Is the 'New Normal' for Millennials: Three Ways to Prevent a Human Resource Nightmare. Retrieved from http://www.forbes.com/sites/jeannemeister/2012/08/14/job-hopping-is-the-new-normal-for-millennials-three-ways-to-prevent-a-human-resource-nightmare/

Park, L. (2003). Numb. *Meteora*.

Reina, D. S., & Reina, M. L. (2006). *Trust and Betrayal in the Workplace*. San Francisco: CA: Berret-Koehler Publishers.

Senge, P., Scharmer, C. O., Jaworski, J., & Flowers, B. S. (2004). *Presence: Human Purpose and the Field of the Future*. New York, NY: Doubleday.

Shih, W., & Allen, M. (2007). Working with generation-D: Adopting and adapting to cultural learning and change. *Library Management, 28*(1), 89–100.

Stress in America Findings. (2010). USA: American Psychological Association.

Suseno, T. (Producer). (2010, October 8, 2013). Jack Welch final GE mgt meeting (1 of 3). [Video] Retrieved from http://www.youtube.com/watch?v=7j5MUPk12Zw

Tjan, A. K. (2012). How Leaders Become Self-Aware. Retrieved from http://blogs.hbr.org/2012/07/how-leaders-become-self-aware/

Tough, P. (2011). What if the Secret to Success Is Failure? *The New York Times*.

Treasurer, B. (2003). *Right Risk: 10 Powerful Principles for Taking Giant Leaps with Your Life*. San Francisco, CA: Berrett-Koehler Publishers.

Treasurer, B. (2011). Courageous Leadership: Participant Workbook. San Francisco, CA: Pfeiffer.

Weiss, T. (2006). Are Parents Killing their Kids' Careers? *Forbes.*

Westerman, J. W., & Yamamura, J. H. (2007). Generational preferences for work environment fit: effects on employee outcomes. *Career Development International, 12*(2), 150 - 161.

Wheatley, M., & Frieze, D. (2011). *Walk Out Walk On: A Learning Journey into Communities Daring to Live the Future Now.* San Francisco, CA: Berrett-Koehler Publishers.

Will you want to hire your own kids? (Will anybody else?). (2009): The Conference Board.

Zemke, R., Raines, C., & Filipczak, B. (2000). *Generations at work: Managing the clash of veterans, boomers, Xers and Nexters in your workplace (2nd ed.).* New York, NY: AMACOM Books.

Open Book Editions
A Berrett-Koehler Partner

Open Book Editions is a joint venture between Berrett-Koehler Publishers and Author Solutions, the market leader in self-publishing. There are many more aspiring authors who share Berrett-Koehler's mission than we can sustainably publish. To serve these authors, Open Book Editions offers a comprehensive self-publishing opportunity.

A Shared Mission

Open Book Editions welcomes authors who share the Berrett-Koehler mission—Creating a World That Works for All. We believe that to truly create a better world, action is needed at all levels—individual, organizational, and societal. At the individual level, our publications help people align their lives with their values and with their aspirations for a better world. At the organizational level, we promote progressive leadership and management practices, socially responsible approaches to business, and humane and effective organizations. At the societal level, we publish content that advances social and economic justice, shared prosperity, sustainability, and new solutions to national and global issues.

Open Book Editions represents a new way to further the BK mission and expand our community. We look forward to helping more authors challenge conventional thinking, introduce new ideas, and foster positive change.

CPSIA information can be obtained at www.ICGtesting.com
Printed in the USA
LVOW11s2052221214

419990LV00002B/4/P